KAMA SUTRA FOR BEGINNERS

Discover The Best Essential Kama Sutra Love Making Techniques !

R. Riley

FREE BONUS INSIDE

3rd Edition

Table of Contents

Introduction

Despite the fact that it's been a part of life since the beginning of mankind, sexual behavior is a topic that is often perceived as a taboo subject in today's society. Yet, the more we run away from it, the more likely we are to encounter problems within our sex lives. Like any other aspect of a relationship, sexual behavior requires openness and communication in order for both parties to be continually satisfied. There's no better way to establish a healthy, satisfying intimate relationship than studying the Kama Sutra.

Anyone who is unfamiliar with the Kama Sutra may be surprised to know that it's actually an ancient text that was developed thousands of years ago. Specifically, it's believed that the Kama Sutra was written anywhere from 400 BCE to 200 CE. It was originally composed in Sanskrit by the Hindu philosopher Vātsyāyana.

Though the Kama Sutra is often regarded as a "sex manual," it is in fact much more about embracing the pleasures of life than about achieving specific sexual positions. In fact, the word "Kama" refers to desire, while "sutra" refers to rules, or the thread that ties all things together. The pursuit of pleasures is known as one of the four aims of life within Hindu traditions. In other words, the Kama Sutra was written as a formula for achieving one's desires.

It is said that the writer of the Kama Sutra, Vātsyāyana, did not believe that sex should be regarded as an off-limits, "bad" behavior; although, he did express the notion that performing sexual acts in a detached, unemotional manner should be considered sinful.

Although the text is ancient by today's standards, the principles found within it are by no means outdated. In fact, it's possible that just about any romantic relationship could benefit by including some of the Kama Sutra ideologies within its sexual endeavors.

Throughout this eBook, we'll explore the ways in which you can implement Kama Sutra practices in your love life to connect on a deeper level with your significant others. Everything from kissing to sexual intercourse can be enhanced so that you can create a more loving, intimate relationship and experience a greater sense of pleasure. You and your loved one can follow along and go at your own pace, exploring the notion of the Kama Sutra in a way that works best for your relationship.

Chapter 1:
History

The history of the Kama Sutra is a long one. It's one of the world's eldest books about pleasure and physical living. There is no solitary author of the text, but it was initially assembled in the third century by Vatsyayana, an Indian sage who lived in the northern part of India. He claimed to be a monk practicing celibacy, and his work in amassing the sexual information of the ages was a way for him to meditate and contemplate the deity. Written in a complex form of Sanskrit, the Kama Sutra is the only remaining text of that era of early Indian history.

In scholarly circles, it's been widely consulted by scholars to determine the social mores and understand the society of that time period. The title of the text translates to a treatise on pleasure. Far more complex than just a listing of the contortionist positions, the Kama Sutra is a all-inclusive handbook of living for the good of life. Although the central character of this work is a man-about-town, the text was written to be read by and provide detailed information for both men and women.

The basic tenant of this book is that in order for a marriage to be happy, both the man and woman have to be well-versed in the art of pleasure, both cerebral and carnal. The topics explored include social concepts, society, sexual union, the acquisition of a wife, about the wife, about the wives of other men, about courtesans, and on the ways to attract others to yourself. The book has detailed advice on what men must do to win over a woman and what a woman must do in order to win over a man, the states of a woman's mind, the role of a go-between, and the reasons why women might reject the advances of a man.

In terms of finding a mate, the Kama Sutra counsels on whether to think about someone from childhood friends or fellow students. It provides diagrams that classify female and male physical types and the compatibility they will have with their lover's body. It teaches varieties of kissing, embracing, biting, scratching, oral sex, and intercourse that are elaborate. The text also has instructions on extramarital relationships, including the wives of other men, and has many pages on how to seduce and extort the courtesan.

Finally, in case all the knowledge in this book should fail in winning the love that a person seeks, the final chapter contains foods, tonics, and powders that have the power to help attract others to that person.

Some refer to this book as the marriage manual, but it's a far cry from the monogamous and dutiful bindings of marriage that Westerns produced as a part of advice for couples. One of the central figures of the book is the courtesan, who must master and practice a variety of arts in order to learn how to please and coerce a man. What is unique about Kama Sutra is that maintains focus on creating pleasure for the woman, too. A man who fails to provide and bring about pleasure to a woman during intercourse will lose her because she will seek it from somewhere else.

Kama Sutra is the original study of sexuality, and so it became the focal point of all proceeding books, including the fifteenth century Ananga-Ranga, which was a revised version that built upon the Vatsyayana's basic beliefs. Yet due to the complex and inaccessible style of Sanskrit in which it was written, the Kama Sutra fell into obscurity for many centuries. Scholars of Sanskrit and ancient Indian did not consult it often. It wasn't until the late nineteenth century that the Kama Sutra began to resume its popularity in Indian.

The resurgence came about after the 1870's when Sir Richard Burton, a noted linguist and Arabic translator, worked with his collaborators to produce a translation of the Ananga-Ranga. When they were pursuing references to the Vatsyayana, they were led back to the Kama Sutra and an English version was produced. Burton's persistence in having this book translated so that Western readers could read it, and the interest the text generated in Indian and abroad, led to a proliferation of translations and versions of this original book.

The Ananga-Ranga was created in the fifteenth century and was an updated version of the Kama Sutra, written in a more understandable Sanskrit that its earlier predecessor. Because of this, for many centuries the Ananga-Ranga superseded the Kama Sutra in being the text of choice to look at for knowledge about sexual pleasure. The writing of this book was ordered by the nobleman Ladakhana for one of the Lodi Dynasty's monarch. This family was a powerful part of Delhi Sultanate, who ruled over the northern part of India before the Mughal Dynasty took over. The author of the Ananga-Ranga, Kalyanamalla was a Hindu poet who referred back to the Kama Sutra heavily in order to prepare his text.

He wrote in an accessible Sanskrit style, and the royal Muslim patronage made sure that the text was circulated around the feudal Muslim kingdoms. Accounts of the Ananga-Ranga now appear in the Persian, Arabic, and Urdu cultures.

The Ananga-Ranga opens with a dedication to Ladakhana, the patron of the text, and contains prescription advice for married couples, and their conduct both socially and sexually. It starts with a detailed description of the woman's body and includes centers of passions, classifications of body types, erogenous zones, and timeliness of their sexual pleasures. Compatibility and classification of men and women by their genital size was explored in numerous combinations and to their degree of passion. Many scholars speculated that Kalyanamalla resided in more sexist civilization than the earlier writers. The noted that Kalyanamalla deviated from the other writers by neglecting to provide normative advice for producing a woman's pleasure, such as the use of fingers, that the other texts reinforce many times. The title of the book, Ananga-Ranga, has been translated to Stage of the Bodiless One, Theatre of the Love God, and The Hindu Art of Love, amongst many others.

As part of the romanticism of colonial rule, Europeans looked for Eastern texts to bring ancient wisdom to their modern world. However, the Orientalist engagement in the Ananga-Ranga led to the text's decreased relevance, and the importance of the previous Kama Sutra. Burton's experience residing in India as part of the British army and his allure with sexual practices, especially those of the Oriental societies, coupled with his desire to bring the knowledge and attention to his peers, led to his interest in the cannon of sexual knowledge that was preserved by the Sanskrit texts.

Because of the seeming popularity of the Ananga-Ranga among many Sanskrit specialists, it was only natural for it to be the text of choice for Burton's purpose. When he reviewed translations, though, he made note of the references that were made to the Vatsyayana. He believed that the earlier text, the Kama Sutra, was a far more foundational piece of work, and requested that a copy be located. Because of its neglect over the centuries, the Kama Sutra only existed in parts. The text had to be remade from Sanskrit manuscript library collections across the Princely States and Indian. Once it was translated into English, its popularity grew, and Indian scholars set aside the Ananga-Ranga with some new interest in the Kama Sutra.

Chapter 2:
Philosophy of Kama Sutra

The idea that Kama Sutra is only the physical aspect of sex is very skewed The purpose of Kama Sutra was not only to educate the masses about different techniques involving sex but to promote a healthy relationship between partners and constructively use sexual energy. Many Western and Indian authors and interpreters have paid very little attention to the other aspects of Kama Sutra. They only pay attention to the physical and sexual parts. However, if you look deeper into the teachings, you can see that Kama Sutra is far beyond just sex.

Let's take a look at some of the other teachings of Kama Sutra that are meant to bring a couple closer together.

Participation

Many of the asanas or positions depicted in Kama Sutra called for active and equal participation of both man and woman.

Rather than sticking to boring and monotonous missionary positions where the woman is a passive receiver, the scripture encourages proactive positions. Only when there is an equal contribution from both ends will the session truly be fruitful and fulfilling. There's no posture that meant exclusively for the man or the woman in Kama Sutra.

The meaning behind this is that whether you are participating in a sexual act or another matter, you should ensure that you are equally involved with your partner. Participation is the keyword here. When you seek an active role from your partner, they feel wanted and there is synergy between the two of you, which leads to greater fulfillment. That's what samabhog or equal pleasure is about.

Body Image vs. The Body

The varied techniques that are described in the scripture make sex pleasurable for anyone no matter what their body type and shape is. The person can be obese, muscular, or thin, but Kama Sutra states that body issues and pleasure are not well mixed.

The message is that you should work on your body image. You can still make the best of the body you have provided you do not have unrealistic expectations of how it should look. Acceptance is the key word here. Magazine covers are flooded with images of bodies that seem perfect, but don't let them fool you. Don't let negative body image spoil your life, whether it is sex or not.

Touch Matters

Kama Sutra lays a lot of importance on touch, and not only during sex. Going by the texts, touch is often varied, each designated to arouse a unique sensation in your partner depending on their likes. However, the role of touch begins in foreplay and continues all the way to the end.

The message here is to not undermine the power of a small touch. That casual hug or the loving caress that's imitated by for the sex says a lot more about your feelings than the actual act. The touch may not even lead to any use, but it's a potent method of conveying emotion. It'll do more good to your relationships than anything else.

Dress to Impress

The scripture emphasizes on shringaar at times and this cannot be undermined. Almost every character that is shown in the act of Kama Sutra wears elaborate ornaments, including the men.

The message here is that while it does depict traditions and cultures of the time that these texts were written, the underlying idea is that you should look good and dress up for your partner. Many couples lose the urge to look good for one another after a few years of courting.

However, that's the wrong idea. Just as you take the effort to dress up for a certain occasion, it's important to look presentable for your partner. Don't undermine the importance of how you look. Get rid of a complacent attitude and communicate to our partner that you are still important.

Play

The Kama Sutra scripture pays a lot of attention and puts a lot of importance on the fun element of sex. That's what converts a boring, mechanical session into something that a couple will look forward to. Try all the experimentation that you want. If the fun element is missing, then there's little that you can do.

The message here is that you should have fun with one another. Start with non-sexual activities and build a rapport. Travel together, play games, discuss movies, and find conversations that are stimulating. When fun is easy, no matter what the occasion is, the joy will be transmitted to other aspects of the relationship by default.

Chapter 3:
Puruṣārtha

Puruṣārtha translates to the object of human pursuit. It's the key concept in Hinduism and references the four proper goals or aims of human life. The four Puruṣārtha are Dharma, Artha, Kama, and Moksha. Dharma translates to moral values, Artha stands for economic values, Kama stands for psychological and pleasure values, and Moksha stands for spiritual values or liberation.

All four of the Puruṣārtha are imperative, but in cases of conflict, Dharma is considered the most important over Kama and Artha, but Moksha is considered the ultimate ideal of human life. Historical scholars recognized and debated the inherent tension between the active pursuit of wealth, pleasure, and the renunciation of all wealth and pleasure for the sake of Moksha. They suggested that nishkam karma was a possible solution to the tension. Nishkam karma is a craving-free action.

Puruṣārtha is a Sanskrit term for Purusha and Artha, with the aforementioned word meaning human being, soul, and universe principle and soul of the universe. The latter of the two words means the object of desire, purpose, and meaning.

Together, the two words mean the purpose of human being. Alf Hiltebeitel translates Puruṣārtha to mean Goals of Man. He clarifies that the word man stands for both woman and man in the early and primitive Indian texts. Olivelle translates the word to mean aims of human life.

Puruṣārtha is an imperative concept in Hinduism, holding that every human being has four goals that are necessary and sufficient in order to fulfill a happy life. These four goals are:

- **Dharma** – this signifies the behaviors that are in accord with rta, the order that makes life and the universe possible. It includes the duties of laws, rights, conduct, virtues, and the right way of living. Hindu Dharma includes religious duties, duties of each individual, and moral rights, as well as the behaviors that enable social order, those that are virtuous, and right conduct. According to Van Buitenen, Dharma is something all human begins must respect and accept in order to sustain harmony and order in the world. It is the pursuit and execution of one's true calling and nature.

- **Artha** – this is the means of life, resources, and activities that enable someone to be in the state they want to be in. It incorporates career, wealth, activity to make a living, economic prosperity, and financial security. The proper pursuit of Artha is considered an important activity of human life in Hinduism.

- **Kama** – this signifies wish, desire, emotions, passion, pleasure of the sense, and the visual enjoyment of affection, life, or love with or without sexual connotations. Kama is love without violating moral responsibility, Artha and one's journey toward spiritual liberation.

- **Moksha** – This signifies a release or emancipation. In some schools of the Hindu ways, Moksha is the freedom from samsara, a cycle of death and rebirth. Sometimes it's viewed as self-knowledge, freedom, and self-realization.

The ancient literature emphasizes that Dharma is the foremost Puruṣārtha. If Dharma is ignored, then Kama and Artha will lead to social chaos. The Apastamba Dharmasutra, Gautama Dharmashastra, and Yajnavalkya Smriti all suggest that Dharma comes first and is more important than the others.

Kama Sutra states that the relative value of three goals is as follows: Artha is more important and should come before Kama, and Dharma is more important and should come before both Kama and Artha. Arthashastra argues that Artha is the foundation of the others. Without prosperity and security at an individual level, both sensuality and moral life become harder. Poverty will breed hate and vice while prosperity will breed love and virtue. This writing also suggests that all three are linked and one should not discontinue to enjoy life, nor honorable behavior, nor the quest of wealth creation. An over pursuit of any one of the aspects of life with a complete rejection of the others will harm all three including the one excessively pursued. The Sastras are relative to age and the pursuit of any of them seems to be different.

Moksha is considered the ultimate goal of human life.

Let's take a look at these in more detail in the following chapters.

Dharma

Dharma translates to protection. By practicing the Hindu teachings, the practitioners protect themselves from suffering the problems of the world. All the problems they experience during daily life originate from ignorance, and the method for eliminating that ignorance is Dharma.

Practicing Dharma is the best method for improving the quality of human life. The quality of life depends not on the external development or material progress, but on the inner development of peace and happiness. For example, in history many Buddhists lived in underdeveloped and poor countries, but they were able to find lasting, pure happiness by practicing what Buddha taught.

If the practitioners integrate Buddha's teachings into their daily lives, they will be able to solve their inner problems and attain a peaceful mind. Without inner peace, outer peace is not possible. If they the practitioner first establishes pace in their minds by training their spiritual paths, outer peace will become natural. But if they do not, world peace is never going to be achieved, no matter how many people want it.

Until now, many people cherished themselves above others, and for as long as they continue to do this, the suffering will not end. However, if the world were to learn to cherish all beings more than they cherished themselves, they would enjoy the bliss of enlightenment. The path to enlightenment is actually very simple, all the world has to do is stop cherishing itself and learn to cherish others. All spiritual realizations would naturally follow this.

So what is self-cherishing?

The instinctive view is that we're all more important than the person standing next to us, whereas the view of the enlightened person is that the others standing next to us are more important. Which of those views do you think would be more beneficial? In life after life, we've been slaves to our self-absorbed viewpoints. We've trusted it and obeyed its every command, believing that the way to solve problems and find happiness was to put ourselves first before everyone else. We've worked hard and long for our own sake, but we don't have much to show for it. We haven't solved our problems and found lasting desire and peace. No, it's clear that pursuing selfish interests has deceived the world. After having indulged in self-absorbed behavior for so many generations, now is the time to realize that it simply doesn't work. Now is the time to switch the object of cherishing from ourselves to our fellow man.

Numerous enlightened people have figured out that by abandoning their self-absorbed ways and cherishing only others, they came to experience real peace and happiness. If we practice the methods they teach, there is no reason why we shouldn't be able to do the same. We can't expect to change our minds overnight, but through consistently and patiently practicing the instructions or cherishing those around us, while at the same time accumulating merit, receiving blessings, and purifying negativity, we can gradually replace our ordinary self-absorbed attitude with a sublime attitude of cherishing our fellow man.

Abandoning Self-Cherishing

So now that you know what self-cherishing or being selfish is, how do you abandon it altogether? To achieve this, we don't need to change our lifestyle, but we do need to change our intentions and views. Our ordinary view is that we're the center of the universe and that other people and things derive their significance from the way in which they affect us. Our car is important because it's ours, and our friends are important because they make us happy. Strangers are not as important because they don't directly affect our happiness, and if a stranger's car is damaged or stolen, we're not as concerned.

As you'll see in later sections, this self-centered view of the world is based on ignorance and does not correspond with our reality. This view is the source of all selfish, ordinary intentions. It's precisely why we believe we're important, need something or deserve something. This is why we engage in negative activities that result in an endless stream of problems for ourselves and others.

By practicing the instructions later in this chapter, you can develop a realistic view of the world that's based on understanding of the equality and interdependence of all living things. Once we view every living thing as important, we'll naturally develop good intentions toward those things. Whereas the mind that cherishes only itself is the basis for all samsaric, impure experiences, and the mind that cherishes other beings is the basis for all good qualities and enlightenment.

Cherishing others is not as difficult as it may seem. All we have to do is understand why we should cherish them and then make a firm decision to do this. Through meditation on that decision, we will develop a deep and powerful feeling of cherishing for every living thing. We then carry this feeling into our daily lives.

Compassion

Having gained experience with cherishing others, you can now extend and deepen your compassion, and the method for doing this is will be revealed here. In general, everyone already has a bit of compassion. Everyone feel compassion when they see their friends or family in distress, even animals feel compassion when they see their offspring is in pain. Compassion is the Buddha-seed or Buddha nature, or out potential to become a Buddha. It's because all living things possess this seed that they will all eventually become a Buddha.

When a dog sees her puppies are in pain, she develops the need to protect them and free them from that pain, and this compassionate wish is the Buddha seed. Unfortunately, animals do not have the ability to develop their Buddha nature. Through meditation, we're able to extend and deepen our compassion until it transforms into the mind of great compassion, a wish to protect all living things without exception from their suffering. Through improving the mind of great compassion, it will eventually transform into the compassion of a Buddha. This actually has the power to protect all living beings. Therefore, the way to become a Buddha is to awaken the compassionate Buddha nature and complete the training in universal compassion. Only people are able to do this.

Compassion is the essence of spiritual life and the main practice of those who devoted their life to attaining enlightenment. It's the origin of the Three Jewels, Dharma, Buddha, and Sangha. It's the origin of Buddha as all Buddhas are made from compassion. It's the origin of Dharma for Buddhas give Dharma traditions driven wholly by the passion for others. It's the root of Sangha because it's by listening to and practicing Dharma teachings that stem from compassion that we become Sangha or superior beings.

So what is compassion?

Compassion is a person who is motivated to cherish other living things and desires to discharge those living things from their sorrow. Sometimes out of selfish intention, we might wish for another person to be free from their suffering. This is common in relationships that are based only on attachment. If our friend is depressed or ill, we may wish them to recover quickly so that we're able to enjoy their company again. But this is still self-centered and is not true compassion. Real compassion is based on treasuring others.

While we at present have some amount of sympathy, it's very prejudiced and partial. When our family and friends are suffering, we easily develop compassion for them but we find it far more difficult to feel that same sympathy for those we find unpleasant or strangers. In addition, we feel compassion for those who experience manifest pain, but not for those who enjoy good conditions, and especially not those who engage in harmful actions.

If we really want to realize our potential by attaining full enlightenment, we have to increase the scope of our compassion until it embrace everything and everyone without exception, just as a mother feels compassion for all her children whether or not they behave well or badly. This universal compassion is the heart of Mahayana Buddhism. Unlike our limited, present compassion, which already comes naturally from time to time, universal compassion has to be cultivated through training over a long period of time.

Cherishing Others

The main reason that may people don't cherish those around them is because they're too preoccupied with themselves and this leaves little room in their minds to appreciate others. If you wish to cherish others sincerely, then you have to reduce your obsessive selfishness. Why is it that people regard themselves as so precious and others are not? It's because we're too familiar with selfishness. Since the beginning of time, we've grasped at a truly existent 'I'. This grasping as ourselves automatically gives rise to selfishness, which makes us instinctively feel we're more important those around us. For ordinary people, grasping at our own self-worth and selfishness feels like we're more important than those around us. The fundamental reason this happens is that our constant familiar with our selfishness day in and day out never ends.

Pride

Since we regard ourselves as so very important and precious, we exaggerate our good qualities and develop and inflated view of ourselves. Almost anything can serve as a basis for our arrogant minds, such as our looks, knowledge, possessions, or status. If we make a witty remark, we think we're clever, or if we travel around the world, we feel that this makes us more fascinating. We can even develop pride on the basis of things we ought to be ashamed of, as our ability to deceive others, or on qualities that we imagine we possess. On the other hand, we find it hard to accept shortcomings and mistakes. We spend so much time thinking about our real or imagined good qualities that we become oblivious to our faults. In reality, our mind is full of delusions but choose to ignore them and may even fool ourselves into thinking that we don't have such repulsive minds. This is like pretending there is no dirt in the house after it's been swept under the carpet.

Admitting Faults

It's often so painful to admit that we have faults that we'll make any excuse rather than alter our exalted view of ourselves. One of the most common ways to not face up to our faults is to blame others. For example, if we have a difficult relationship with someone, we will logically determine that it's entirely their responsibility. We're unable to accept that it's at least partly ours. Instead of taking accountability for our actions and making an effort to change our behavior, we argue with that persona and insist that it's they who have to change.

An exaggerated sense of our importance leads to a critical attitude toward others and makes it impossible to avoid conflict. The fact that we're oblivious to our faults doesn't prevent others from noticing them and pointing them out, but when they do we feel that they're unfair. Instead of looking honestly at our behavior to see whether or not the criticism is justified, our self-absorbed mind becomes defensive and retaliates by finding faults in them.

Don't Look For Faults in Others

Another reason we don't regard others as being precious as we are is that we pay attention to their faults while we ignore their good qualities. Unfortunately, we've become skilled in recognizing the faults of others, and we devote a lot of mental energy and time to list them, analyze them, and even meditate on them. With this critical attitude, if we disagree with a colleague or partner about something, instead of attempting to understand their point of view, we repeatedly think of reason as to why we're right and they're wrong. By focusing exclusively on their faults and limitations, we become resentful and angry, and rather than cherish them, we develop the wish to discredit or harm them. In this way, small disagreements can easily turn into a conflict that will simmer for months.

Dharma is about letting go of ourselves and accepting others for who they are. It's about seeing the good in people and ignoring their faults. It's about realizing that we have faults and goodness to us and that we should work on our faults before we point the finger at others. Dharma is about having compassion and empathy for those around us, and cherishing all lives as they should be cherished.

Now that you know more about the teachings of the Dharma let's move on to Artha.

Artha

Artha translates to goal, meaning, sense, purpose, or essence depending on the context it's used in. It's a broader concept in the scriptures of Hinduism. Like the concept, Artha has multiple meanings, all of which translates to the meaning of life, resources, and activities that enable a person to be in the state they want to be in.

Artha applies to both the individual and to the government. The individual context, it includes career, wealth, activity to make a living, economic prosperity, and financial security. The right pursuit of Artha is considered an important aim of life in Hinduism. At the government level, Artha includes legal, social, and worldly economic affairs. Proper Arthashastra is considered an imperative and necessary objective of government.

In the Hindu tradition, Artha is connected to the three aspects and goals of human life known as Kama, Dharma, and moksha. Together, they form the aims of life known as Puruṣārtha.

Meaning

Artha as a concept has many different meanings. It's difficult to capture the meaning of this concept or related terms in a single English word.

Artha has been described as the means of life and include material prosperity. It's also been described as an attitude and capability that enables a person to make a living, remain alive, and to thrive as a free person. It includes economic prosperity, health, and security of a person and those they feel responsible for. It includes everything in a person's environment that allows them to live. It's neither an end state nor an endless goal of aimlessly gathering money. Rather, it's an attitude and necessary requirement o human life.

The central philosophy or premise of Hindu is that everyone should live a joyous and pleasurable life, and such fulfilling of this type of life requires that everyone's needs and desires should be acknowledged and fulfilled. Their needs can only be satisfied through activity and when the proper means are available for those activities.

History

The word Artha appears in the oldest known scriptures of India. However, the term means goal, purpose, or aim for something that's as a purpose of ritual sacrifices. Over time, it evolves into a broader concept during the Upanishadic era. It's first included as part of the Trivarga concept, which expanded into the concept of Caurvarga or Puruṣārtha.

Ancient literature has emphasized that Dharma is the foremost of the four Puruṣārtha, and if Dharma is ignored, then Artha and Kama will only lead to social chaos.

Vatsyayana, the author of Kama Sutra, recognized the relative value of the three objectives as follows: Artha was more significant and should go before Kama, but Dharma was more significant and should come before both Kama and Artha. Arthashastra, another ancient text, argues that Artha is the foundation for the other two Puruṣārtha. Without security and prosperity in society or at the individual level, both sensuality and moral life become difficult. Poverty is something that breeds hate and vice and prosperity breeds love and virtue. Kautilya, the author of Arthashastra, also argues that all three are mutually connected and one should not stop loving life or virtuous behavior or the search for wealth creation. Disproportionate quest of any one aspect of life is going to reject the other two, and this harms all three, even the one excessively pursued.

Therefore, it's important to find your calling in life and to follow it, but it's also important to follow the other two Puruṣārtha, love, and compassion.

Kama

Kama translates to wish, desire, and longing in Hindu culture. It often is meant to mean sexual desire and longing in contemporary literature, but the concept more often refers to wish, desire, longing, passion, pleasure of the senses, and the aesthetic enjoyment of life with or without sexual implications.

Kama is one of the four goals of the Hindu traditions. It's considered an essential and healthy goal of human life when pursued without sacrificing the other three goals.

In Hinduism, Kama is looked at as one of the four proper and necessary goals of human life. Ancient Indian teachings emphasized Dharma has to come first and was essential. If Dharma was ignored, then Artha and Kama led to social chaos.

Necessary for Existence

Just as good food is necessary for the well-being of our physical body, good pleasure is necessary for the healthy existence of a human. A life without enjoyment and pleasure, artistic, sexual, or nature, is a hollow and empty existence. Just as no one should stop farming crops though everyone knows there are herds of deer existing and willing to eat the crops they grow, in the same ways, one should not discontinue their pursuit of Kama just because hazards exist. Kama should be followed with care, thought, enthusiasm, and caution, just as farming or any other life pursuit would be followed.

Kama Sutra is presumed to be a synonym or depicted as creative sexual positions, but only twenty percent of the teachings of this book are actual sex positions. The majority of the book is about the philosophy and theory of love, what triggers our desire, what sustains it, how and when it's good or bad. It's an essential and joyful aspect of the human existence.

Vatsyayana writes that Kama is never in conflict with Artha or Dharma, rather that the three coexist and Kama is a result of the other two. Someone who practices Dharma, Artha, and Kama will enjoy happiness in the present and the future. Any action that is conducive to the practice of Dharma, Kama, and Artha together or of any two or one of them should be performed. But an action that is conducive to the practice of one of them at the expense of the other should not be performed.

In Hindu philosophy, pleasure, whether it's sexual or not, is neither dirty nor shameful. It's a necessary action for human life, essential to the well-being of every persona, and wholesome when it's pursued in its due consideration of Artha and Dharma. Unlike many other teachings of other religions, Kama is celebrated and has a value in its own right. Together with Dharma and Artha, it's an aspect of a holistic life. All three Puruṣārtha are important and equal.

Some ancient literature observes that the relative precedence of Kama, Artha, and Dharma are naturally different for each individual and different age groups. As a child or baby, education and Kama are more important, in youth, Artha and Kama are more important, and as old age takes over, Dharma is the one that takes the lead.

Kama is the experience of the divine using the senses. It's a vehicle returning home to the self. If you want to use Kama in a productive way in your daily life, try out some of these activities:

- Make a list of your desires and figure out which ones are important to you. Figure out which one have been fulfilled and which ones need some more time.

- Evaluate your different desires and see which ones will serve you and which ones will cause suffering and pain.

- Allow yourself to become devoted to a deity that you're drawn to through meditations or mantras.

- Experience the manifestation of divinity using the senses such as mantra, candlelight, sacred images, spiritual music, and incense.

- Experience divinity through nature.

- Study and contemplate the sacred texts.

- Being the practice of Ayurveda or yoga.

- Begin a meditation practice you do daily.

- Practice giving to others.

- Recognize that Kama is a force that's powerful in your life. Examine that ways you can use it to be positive, productive, and balanced.

- Realize that it's a goal in life that will lead to the manifestation of moksha or liberation.

- Create a list of things you value and cultivate them using some of the techniques you've learned.

- Make a positive sensory input.

Moksha

In Indian philosophy and religion, Moksha is also known as mukti, vimoksha, and vimukti. It stands for liberation, emancipations or release. In the eschatological and soteriological sense, it stands for freedom from samsara, the cycle of death and rebirth. In the epistemological and psychological sense, moksha means self-realization, freedom, and self-knowledge.

In the Hindu tradition, moksha is a central concept that is included as one of the four goals and aspects of human life. The concept of moksha can be found in Buddhism, Jainism, and Hinduism. In some schools of Indian religion, moksha is considered interchangeable with terms like kaivalya, vimukti, vimoksha, mukti, apavarga, and nirvana. However, terms like moksha and nirvana differ in their meaning in different schools of Hinduism, Jainism, and Buddhism. The term nirvana is found more common in Buddhism and moksha is more prevalent in Hinduism.

Moksha is viewed as the final release from a person's worldly conception of self, the loosening of the shackle of observed duality and knowledge of one's own fundamental nature which is true being, bliss, and pure consciousness. At liberation, the person's atman or self is realized to be with the ground of all being.

The self as an individual is understood to have never existed. Moksha can involve forsaking everything materials and establishing your existence as a purely devoted servant of Vishnu. The practice of Bhakti Yoga is one of the ways to reach Moksha. There are four different practices that need to be mastered.

The first is Jñāna Yoga or the way of knowledge. The second is mārga or the way of loving devotion. The third is Karma Yoga or the way of works. The fourth is Raja Yoga, the way of meditation and contemplation.

Let's take a look at all four so that you know how to perform them. You'll want to learn some of the basics of the path to moksha because it will help you as you perform Kama Sutra.

Jñāna Yoga

Jñāna yoga is the yoga of knowledge, but not in the intellectual sense. It's the knowledge of Atman and Braham, and the realization of their unity. Where someone who is devoted to

God follows the promptings of their heart, the jnani uses the power of the mind to discriminate between reality and the unreal.

Jnanis, or followers of the advaita Vedanta, are also called monists because they affirm the sole reality of Braham. Therefore, all followers of Vedanta are monists. The distinction is that of spiritual practice. While the Vedantins are theoretically monistic, in practice, those who are devoted to God prefer to think of God as distinct from themselves in order to enjoy the relationship. Jnanis believe that duality is ignorance. There is no need to look outside of the person for divinity; we are already divine.

Hindus believe that there is a veil that prevents us from knowing our true nature and the nature of those around us, and it's known as the veil of maya. Jñāna yoga is the process of pulling away that veil.

The first part of understanding Jñāna is negative. It's the process of neti, neti or not this, not this, meaning that whatever is unreal is rejected. The second part is positive, so whatever is understood to be eternal and unchanging is accepted as being real in the highest sense.

What the teachings are saying is that the universe as we see it is unreal and the universe as we see is not the ultimate reality.

The idea is that what we take in throughout bodily senses, our minds, our intellects is restricted by the nature of our minds and bodies. Braham is infinite, and cannot be restricted. Therefore, the universe we see is not the infinite, powerful Braham. The minds are bounded by the possible condition, whatever the mind and intellect see cannot be the infinite fullness of Braham. Braham has to be beyond what the normal mind can comprehend, it is beyond speech and mind.

Yet what we perceive cannot be anything other than Braham because Braham is infinite and eternal. Jnanis forcefully removes the misperception through the negative process of discrimination between reality and fiction using the positive approach of self-affirmation.

Self-Affirmation

In the process of self-affirmation, the practitioner continuously affirms what is real about themselves, such as: they are not limited to their physical body, they are not limited by their minds, they are spirit, they were never born and will never die, and they are perfect, pure, free, and eternal. That's the greatest truth of our existence.

The philosophy behind self-affirmation is very simple. While you think, so you become. We've programmed ourselves for thousands of lifetimes to think that we're puny, limited, weak, and helpless. This is a terrible life and very self-destructive. It's the worst poison imaginable. If we believe we are weak, then we will act weak. If we believe we are helpless, then we will act helpless. If we believe we are pure, free, and perfect, then we will act pure, free and perfect.

As we've driven the wrong thoughts into our minds repeatedly to create the wrong impression, we must now reverse the process by driving the right impressions into our brains of purity, strength, and truth.

Jñāna yoga uses these considerable mental powers to end the duping process.

Bhakti Yoga

Bhakti yoga is mārga or the way of love and devotion.

For those who are more emotional than they are intellectual, they should try Bhakti yoga. This is the path of devotion and the method used to attain God through love and the loving recollection of God. Most religions emphasize a spiritual path because it is the most natural. As with any other yoga, the goal of Bhakta is to attain God-realization or oneness with the divine. Bhakta helps you attain this through the force of love, the most irresistible and powerful of emotions.

Love is available to everyone. Everyone has loved something or someone with great intensity. Love makes you forget yourself, your whole attention being devoted to that object of your adoration. The ego will loosen its grip as you think of the welfare of your beloved one, and love gives you concentration, even against your will. You always remember the object of your life. In an easy and completely painless way, love makes the preconditions necessary for a good spiritual life.

You should never squander the power of love. Use this force for finding the divine. You have to remember that when you love another you are really responding unconsciously to the divinity within that person. Our love for others is unselfish and motiveless when we're able to encounter the divinity in them.

Unfortunately, people have a tendency to misplace their love. They project their vision of what's perfect, true, and beautiful and impose that on whatever or whomever they love. It is only God alone who is all those things. Therefore, you should put the emphasis back where it belongs, on the divine self in every person that you come across. That is the real object of your love.

Recognize the divinity in the other person and focus on that rather than their limitedness as a person.

Karma Yoga

This form of yoga is the action of work. Specifically, it's the path of dedicated work. It's renouncing the results of your actions as a spiritual offering rather than hoarding the results to yourself.

Karma is both action and the result of the action. What you experience today is the result of your karma, both bad and good, created by your previous actions. This chain of action and reaction you've created can be snapped by karma yoga. It's basically fighting fire with fire and using the sword of karma yoga to stop the chain reaction of action and reaction. By disengaging your ego from the work process and offering the results to a higher power, you stop the snowballing process.

Whether you realize it or not, everyone performs actions constantly. Sitting and thinking are both actions. Reading is an action. Action is something that cannot be stopped. It's a part of who are and what we have to do to stay alive.

All of us tend to work with an expectation in mind. We work hard at our careers to get appreciation and respect from colleagues and promotions from our boss. We clean the yard and make it look wonderful with the hope that neighbors will be appreciative or envious or our work. We work hard at school to get good grades in the hopes that this will bring us a fine future. We cook a nice meal with the expectation that someone will praise and applaud us. We dress nicely in the hopes that someone notices. So much of our lives are run expecting the future results that we do it unconsciously and automatically.

However, this is a perilous pattern. From the spiritual viewpoint, all the anticipations and expectations are the Trojan horse that will bring us pain rather than joy. Misery is inevitable because desires and expectations are unappeasable and unending. We live from disappointment to disappointment because our motivation is only to enlarge and gratify our ego. We forge the fresh chains of karma rather than breaking the bonds.

No matter whether you're devotional, meditative, or intellectual in your personality, karma yoga is easily practiced in tandem with the other spiritual paths. Even those who lead a meditative life benefit from karma yoga, for thoughts are able to produce bonds just as any physical action can.

Just as devotees offer incense and flowers in their loving worship to their God, so can actions and thoughts be offered as worship of the divine.

Raja Yoga

This is the royal path of meditation. As a king would maintain control over his kingdom, so can you maintain control over your 'kingdom'. The vast territory of the mind is your kingdom. In raja yoga, you use mental powers to realize Atman through the process of psychological control.

The basic premise of this teaching is that your perception of the divine self is hidden by disturbances of your mind. If your mind can be made to stay pure and still, the self will instantaneously shine forth.

If you can imagine a lake that is whipped with waves, fouled by pollution or muddied by tourists, then you'll get a fair assessment of the mind's slate.

If you don't believe this assertion, then try meditating upon the Atman for a while. A thousand different thoughts will fly at you, all leading your mind outward. The fly buzzing around is suddenly very important. So is the thought of dinner. You'll now remember where you left those car keys. The argument you had yesterday is more vivid and powerful than it was when it happened. The minute you stop thinking one thought, another thought will jump in with equal force.

Most of the time, people are unaware of their mind's unpredictable actions because they are habituated to giving their minds free reign. They are never really tempted to observe, let alone train their mind. Like parents whose lack of discipline has created turbulent, ill-behaved children, our minds behave badly.

Without having psychological discipline, the mind is a mental equivalent of a house ape. And all of us are suffering mental agony because of it.

Mastering Your Mind

While many are accustomed to living with an uncontrolled mind, we should not assume that it's acceptable. You can master your mind and through repeated practice you can make the mind your servant rather than the beginnings of a victim. The mind, when it's trained, is the truest friend. When it's left untrained, it's reckless and an enemy.

Now rather than envisioning that polluted lake, think of a clear, beautiful lake with no pollution, no waves, no tourist, and no speedboats. It's as clear as glass. It's tranquil, calm, and quiet. Now as you look down through the pure water, you can see the bottom of the lake. The bottom, metaphorically, is the Atman that's deep inside your heart. When the mind is calm and pure, the self is no longer hidden from your view.

The mind is cleansed and made peaceful through the repeated process of meditation and through the practice of moral virtues. Popular belief aside, there is no way to practice meditation without practicing the moral virtues at the same time. To try to do this another way is as effective as trying to start a car without a battery.

For this task, all areas of the mind have to be fully engaged. You cannot compartmentalize your life and assume that you can have both a secular area and a spiritual area. Just as you cannot start a car without a battery, you cannot cross the ocean with your legs on two different boats. You must fully integrate all aspects of your life and direct your energy toward one goal.

This doesn't that in order to realize God you have to totally renounce the world and live in a convent or monastery, but you do have to direct all aspects of your life toward spiritualization so that you can be directed to the goal of moksha.

Because raja yoga is the path of meditation, it's generally followed by those who are happy leading a contemplative life. Most will never fall into that category. However, Raja Yoga is an essential component to the other paths and teachings because meditation is involved in the loving recollection of God, mental discrimination, and an essential balance to selfless action.

Meditation

As for direction on how to meditate and what to meditate on, such issues have to be taken up with a qualified leader. Meditation is a very personal matter, and only a genuine spiritual guide can accurately gauge your personal tendencies and direct your mind accordingly.

In addition, spirituality cannot be taught, it is something you learn on your own. A genuine spiritual teacher will ignite the flame, and the student will have to obtain their own attainment. Your candle cannot be lit by a book any more than it can be lit by an unqualified teacher who speaks religion without living it. True spirituality is transmitted, and only unselfish, pure teachers who have achieved a level of spiritual awakening can enliven your dormant flame.

That being said, there was some basic guidelines that you can follow and find in other resources to help you get started.

So how does Puruṣārtha help you in your love life? When all the Puruṣārtha are mastered, you are a person who is able to see the divine in their partner, respect them, and you are able to understand that your love for them is truly the love of the divine. Puruṣārtha helps you become a better love through having compassion, empathy, and love for the person you are with. When you have that, you will show your lover nothing but kindness. This makes for an attentive partner in the bedroom.

Chapter 4:
Benefits of Kama Sutra

Just like with any relationship, there are benefits to having physical contact, but there are specific benefits when it comes to Kama Sutra foreplay and sex. You see, Kama Sutra is not just about the positions, but about the foreplay involved and the different stages it takes to lead up to the mind-blowing experience of Kama Sutra positions. So what are the direct benefits of learning Kama Sutra?

Variety of Positions

Your sex life is never going to get boring when there are sixty-nine original sex positions to learn from! Many of those positions will be described in this book so that you can find what pleases both you and your partner.

Every Aspect of Sex

Rather than just teach you the positions that you can try out, Kama Sutra teaches you all about the different aspects of sex. You'll learn about how to apply romance, foreplay, sex, and after play to your sex life for a more rounded experience!

Makes You More Attractive to the Opposite Sex

Kama Sutra teaches you what another person needs both physically and mentally before, during, and after sex. It also tells you how to fulfill those needs! Setting the mood for a proper evening and knowing that you are prepared for an evening with someone else boosts your confidence, which helps boost your attractiveness with the opposite sex.

Teaches You Cunnilingus and Fellatio

Men and women tend to go about giving and receiving oral sex the same way every time. While some of them might be experts at these two ways to perform oral sex, most could do with knowing a few more tips. The tips and techniques that Kama Sutra explains for oral sex are ones that will have partners begging for more! Your partner is going to love that you are trying to please them and heighten their arousal, and you are going to love that they want to do the same for you.

Gives You Confidence

If you're looking to be the sex god or goddess that your partner wants to be with, you might want to consider adding some enhancement supplements to your diet. There is nothing wrong with trying to be healthier and last longer for your partner. This will give you more confidence in the end, and that will give both you and your partner a better time in bed.

Anti-Aging Properties

You read that right. Kama Sutra helps promote anti-aging properties in the body. It creates a strong bond between you and your partner and is a great way to boost both beauty and vitality. Those who have regular sex are less likely to have heart disease and arthritis. They're also said to live a longer life than those who abstain from sex.

Practicing unique positions on a daily basis helps ensure that your body stays slim and you are glowing from the inside out. This is due to hormonal functions being proper rather than falling to the wayside due to inactivity. The muscles are also stimulated during the act of sex, which helps keep them mobile and fit. In addition to that, the heart pumps blood to all areas of the body during sex and this helps keep the body healthier.

Kama Sutra sex positions have been practiced across the globe. They've gone through the medieval times and are still practiced in the modern times. They not only give couples physical enjoyment but have many other benefits attached to them.

So how can you have quality sex every time you have sex with your partner?

Follow these tips to find out more.

- **Communication:** Just like every other aspect of your relationship, having good communication is going to make your sex life excellent both in and out of the bedroom. You want to have good communication not only during sex but while the two of you are just out and about doing chores or running errands. You need to satisfy your wants and desires, and you need to tell your partner how you require that you're loved. Find out what you want from yourself and then discuss what you want with your partner, and don't forget to ask what they want and really listen!

- **Add Flavor:** Monotonous sex is boring for both you and your partner. No one wants to have the same sex day in and day out. Before intercourse, show your partner areas where you want to become aroused; have them show you how they want to become aroused. Talk dirty, take food into the bedroom like butter, chocolate, and strawberry to enhance the foreplay, put on some soft music, and put some flowers around the room. The ambiance needs to be arousing and sexy, and make sure that no one can disturb the two of you!

- **Learn About Positions:** Couples who are more adventurous and try out more positions are more likely to be happy in bed. You can also try adding flavored condoms, lubricant, and toys to the bedroom to spice things up. Try different positions and watch movies together to arouse each other and learn more about the positions that you can tray, and of course, try out the positions that you find in this book!

- **Stay Physically Active:** Let's face it, as you get older, you start to forget about keeping your body in shape and worry about the other woes of life. But what about what your partner wants, and don't you want to feel sexy in bed? Sex is a vigorous form of exercise and it's necessary to be in good health when having great sex. Not only is your partner going to enjoy having more sex, but they're going to enjoy the benefits the both of you will gain.

So now that you know more about the benefits of having Kama Sutra sex and just more sex, in general, let's talk about some of the foreplay you can enjoy with your partner, starting with kissing.

Chapter 5:
Kissing

When kissing comes to mind, one might imagine that the act of locking lips should be pretty straightforward. After all, kissing has been regarded as a symbol of love, seemingly since the beginning of mankind. It's typically the first indication that a relationship is progressing to a more romantic level, and when done properly, it should send both parties into a state of passion, desire, and excitement.

What do we mean by "properly?" Again, you may think that as long as you've done it enough times, you know all there is to know about the act of kissing. Unless you're an expert on the Kama Sutra, though, that most likely isn't true. Here's why: within the Kama Sutra, there are multiple different ways to kiss your lover, including the pressed kiss, the straight kiss, and the turned kiss.

Oftentimes, we fall into specific patterns when it comes to our love lives, either because we've become comfortable in our routines or because we're hesitant to try new things. This happens quite often in relationships that have been ongoing for at least a few years, but it doesn't have to be that way. If you and your loved one are interested in exploring different techniques, you shouldn't hold back. Kissing should not be done complacently - like other aspects of physical touch, it's important to try to express your emotions and passions through the delivery of your kiss. Likewise, you should be the recipient of passion when you are kissed back.

In addition to acting as a gateway to further romantic physical activity within a relationship, kissing is also an essential element of foreplay. In other words, kissing should, in some way, take place before you and your partner engage in lovemaking, regardless of how long you've been together or how rushed the act may be. Oftentimes, outside factors get in the way of a couple's love lives; jobs, families, and other stressors can make it difficult to find the time or peace of mind for sex. Yet, a couple shouldn't rely on simply going through the motions each time they engage in sexual activity. Instead, they should bring passion into the mix each time they make love. One way to ensure that is by practicing Kama Sutra kissing techniques.

Perhaps the most common kissing technique is the bent kiss. In order to achieve this type of kiss, each party bends his or her head towards the other. The kissing takes place as the heads are bent at an angle.

The straight kiss is another common kissing technique. The Kama Sutra describes it as a kiss in which both lovers' lips are brought directly towards one another. This kiss works for some couples better than it does for others. Just be sure to avoid injuring your noses if you use this kissing method.

The turned kiss is considered to be a bit more passionate. In this technique, one person turns his or her head up to face the other individual, and the other individual typically will hold the head of that person. The added touch of the chin can be very sensual and can add an element of lust to an ordinary kiss. If you'd like to try out the turned kiss and you're the taller person in your relationship, place your hand gently under the chin of your loved one to tilt his or her head up, and then bestow a kiss. If you would like to be the recipient of the turned kiss or you're the shorter individual, you can encourage your partner to place his or her hand on your chin by grabbing his hand and placing it where you'd like it to be; or, you could always simply ask him or her to do it. Keep in mind that you or your partner's height doesn't have to be the determining factor for engaging in this type of kiss - one of you could always sit while the other stands.

Another passionate method of Kama Sutra kissing is the pressed kiss. In this variation, one person presses the other individual's lower lip with great force, using both of his or her lips. To try this on your lover, pucker his or her bottom lip out slightly using your index finger immediately prior to your kiss.

Keep in mind that any of these kissing variations can lead to tongue kissing. Referred to in the Kama Sutra as "the fighting for the tongue," this form of kissing takes place when either party's tongue touches the other individual's teeth, palate, or tongue. Typically, this type of open-mouthed kissing has the potential to lead to further sexual activity.

Most importantly, make sure to always include kissing in your sexual repertoire. Overlooking the act of kissing can make a lovemaking experience dull and disconnected. Feel free to experiment with the techniques listed above for unique and new approaches to kissing that will kick start your sexual experience with your loved one.

Chapter 6:
Touching

Sometimes, passionate kissing leads directly to lovemaking. Yet, oftentimes, further foreplay takes place in the form of touching. Touching is can be emotive and extremely powerful: it has the potential to send shivers across one's skin, or even bring your lover to the point of orgasm depending on where you touch him or her. The amount of time you spend on touching will ultimately be up to you and your partner, but more often than not, it's an essential aspect of foreplay that has the potential to greatly improve your sex life.

While the Kama Sutra outlines specific types of embraces, it also encourages loved ones to partake in sensual touching or even massaging. For starters, it's important to understand where your partner likes to be touched. Using a light, sensual touch, explore the areas of his or her body, making your way from the lips down to the lower regions. Despite the fact that there are known erogenous zones (or areas of the body with extra sensitivity), each person's body is different.

The erogenous zones are particularly sensitive because they contain a high concentration of nerve endings; yet, these places are pleasurable for some more so than others. For instance, some people can become aroused when areas on their upper bodies, including eyelids, temples, shoulders, hands, hair, and arms are touched. Others enjoy the sensation of their earlobes being touched. Moving downwards, the nipples and navel can be quite sensitive to touch, so take extra care to experiment with different forms of touching in these areas.

Spots of the legs, such as the inner thigh, can be extremely sensitive. Of course, the genitals are the most obvious erogenous zones. Nonetheless, some individuals are much more sensitive than others. For instance, some women require very light, and perhaps even indirect touching on or around the clitoris, while others can tolerate a more intense level of pressure.

Experiment with different types of touches across your partner's body. Some areas may require gentle, smooth strokes, while in other areas, you may be able to use a greater amount of force.

In addition to regular touching using hands or fingertips, the Kama Sutra offers some advice on biting and scratching. While it regards these practices as indicators of intense lovemaking sessions, it does recommend that they be reserved only for those who find it pleasurable. As with any other bedroom behavior, both parties must take enjoyment in the act in order for it to be worthwhile. If you plan to experiment with roughness, consider adopting a "code" word - many couples choose to use the word "red" or another color - to indicate that you're experiencing too much pain. Or, you could implement a warning word, such as "orange" to let your partner know that he or she is on the threshold of becoming too rough.

The Kama Sutra also encourages various means of foreplay, including bathing together. This allows you to explore one another's bodies and try out different touching techniques with the added element of water. It changes things up a bit from the traditional bedroom setting, and you can also experiment with different materials, such as a wash cloth or sponge.

When bathing together, don't make it a mission to scrub each other clean or perform a routine hair washing. Instead, focus on touching one another. From there, you can either choose to make love right in the shower, or move things to the bedroom. Be cautious with the wet surfaces, though, and take care not to slip.

Embracing is another important aspect of initiating passion amongst a couple. The Kama Sutra outlines more than ten different types of embraces. These positions can be achieved prior to, during, or after sexual intercourse. Most importantly, the majority of these embraces encourage direct eye contact, so that partners can feel connected to each other while partaking in physical touch.

The touching embrace, according to the Kama Sutra, takes place when a man's body is placed in front or alongside a woman, and his body touches hers. The rubbing embrace occurs when a couple is walking next to one another, and their bodies make contact as they do so. If one party presses the other's body up against a wall or another structure, that's known as the pressing embrace.

The piercing embrace is more sexual than the others we've listed above. A female can achieve this movement by rubbing her breast against a male while he's either sitting or standing. The man then takes hold of her breasts, thereby initiating sexual touching. If you've never attempted this approach, it can be a fun, unique way to encourage foreplay.

The woman can also initiate an embrace called "climbing a tree." The Kama Sutra describes this movement as an act in which the woman keeps one foot on the ground or atop her lover's foot, and wraps the other leg around his leg. In essence, she is "climbing" her lover. This is another inventive way to approach foreplay or lovemaking, and it can become very sensual very quickly for both parties.

One of the most sensual - and potentially arousing - embraces is the milk and water embrace. This occurs when a man sits on a chair or on the edge of a bed, and the woman sits on his lap facing him, so that their torsos can be pressed against one another. The milk and water position can easily lead to intercourse, due to its positioning.

There are also embraces that the Kama Sutra encourages in the lying down position. For one, there's the embrace of the thighs, in which one lover presses the other's thighs between his or her own. Another well-known embrace is that of the jaghana. In this pose, a man presses the woman's jaghana (area between his navel and thighs) to his own and lays atop her, to ether kiss or touch her. Oftentimes, couples take a variation of this position prior to lovemaking, but consider implementing this technique by pressing your pelvises together for added intensity during foreplay.

While you can play around with any of these touches, embraces, and explorations of the erogenous zones, keep in mind that regardless of whichever method you choose, the act of touching is essential to achieving passion in your love life.

Chapter 7:
Kissing the Body

As we explained in the previous chapters, there are certain spots within the body that are especially sensitive and can provide great pleasure when touched. Yet, instead of just touching, you can also take it a step further and concentrate on these areas using your mouth. Love and passion should involve exploration. Even if you've been in a committed monogamous relationship for a long period of time, the act of engaging in foreplay should never get "old," because there are always new techniques and places to test out.

If you're unsure of where or how to begin, consider placing light, gentle kisses on your lover's upper body, and then make your way down from there. For instance, if you're already engaging in kissing, you might want to migrate to your partner's neck, and move slowly towards his or her ear, and go from there. Oftentimes, people tend to focus their attention on the front side of the body; however, the upper back, shoulder blades, and nape of the neck can be extremely sensitive.

Kissing these areas can be extremely arousing for some individuals.

In fact, the Kama Sutra encourages bestowing a row of kisses along your loved one's spine. The spine is typically overlooked, yet, it's known as the life line of our bodies. Why not experiment with touching and kissing this sensual area?

Keep in mind that you don't need to approach kissing the body the same way that you might approach kissing your lover's mouth. You can even run your lips sensually over your partner's skin, breathe warmly in his or her tender areas, or grab his or her skin with your lips. Nibbling, sucking, and licking are all fair game, too - as long as your partner seems to be enjoying what you're doing.

This is another instance in which providing vocal feedback can become helpful. Encourage your partner to tell you what he or she likes, and return the favor by giving vocal cues when he or she does something that you enjoy.

Of course, there are areas you may want to focus on specifically. Using your mouth on your loved one's genitals to satisfy him or her can be erotic and extremely pleasurable. Yet, it's not uncommon for couples to ease back on, or stop oral pleasure altogether after they've been together awhile. They find a routine in which they can both become satisfied, and sex becomes a regular everyday activity, instead of an act of great passion and arousal. There's nothing wrong with sticking with what you like, but you and your loved one will benefit by keeping things exciting. Returning to oral pleasure, at least every now and then, can be an unexpected, pleasant surprise for your loved one if you haven't done it in a while.

While your technique will ultimately be dictated by what your partner enjoys, there are certain methods you can use that tend to be quite pleasurable for most people.

In terms of performing fellatio, there are several techniques adapted by the Kama Sutra that men, in general, tend to find pleasurable. The Kama Sutra encourages individuals performing fellatio to imagine "sucking on a mango fruit." To do this, one may wish to use various techniques, including licking the penis in upward directions, flicking the tongue along the ridge on the underside of the penis, gently nibbling the sides of the shaft, and sucking vigorously. Remember that each man is different, and what may be pleasing to one individual could be painful to another. Encourage your partner to be vocal about what feels good and what doesn't.

There are also various options for performing cunnilingus that women may find enjoyable. The Kama Sutra refers to this sexual act as "licking a delicate flower," but does not go into great detail about specific techniques. Nonetheless, there are some methods inspired by the text that seem to work well for many couples. Most women enjoy the sensation of having the clitoris stimulated; yet, keep in mind that this is the most sensitive spot of a woman's body. Oftentimes, it's best to start out gently, and if your partner responds positively, apply more pressure. You may want to begin by using both your lips and tongue; from there, you can progress to more intense motions, such as flicking the tongue. You can also kiss and lick the labia, and explore the vagina by inserting your finger or tongue. Some women enjoy this sensation; again, though, all women are different, so pay attention to the ways in which your partner responds to your various techniques.

Of course, both parties can be engaged in oral pleasure through the position known as "the crow." According to the

Kama Sutra this takes place when both lovers are simultaneously performing oral sex on one another. It's also commonly referred to as "69-ing." Implement the same techniques described above, but don't forget to pay attention to the pleasure that you're receiving at the same time!

Chapter 8:
Positions for Beginners

If you've been a part of a long-term, committed relationship, it's likely that you and your partner have already explored a few different sexual positions. You may know what feels best for one another, and what helps both parties to achieve climax most effectively. Yet, simply returning to the same positions time after time can make sex less exciting.

Whether you've stuck to the same sexual positions for most of your life, or you've just been stuck in the same routine for quite some time, it can be beneficial for both you and your partner to explore the different sex positions outlined by the Kama Sutra. Try the positions listed below for starters, and as you progress, consider experimenting with some of the more advanced moves, which we'll describe in the following chapter.

Side-By-Side Clasping Position

In this sex position, the man and woman are lying next to one another, looking into each other's faces. Their bodies are tilted towards one another, and the man will enter the woman as they continue to lay facing each other. For best results, the woman may want to hook her leg over the top leg of the man.

Rocking Horse

This is a variation of the classic woman-on-top sex position. Instead of lying down, the man will sit cross-legged and support himself with his hands as he leans back a bit. The woman kneels over the man's lap and lowers herself onto him, hugging his body with her thighs. This position may be easier for both parties if the man chooses to lean his back against a wall or other support system.

Glowing Triangle

The glowing triangle is easy for beginners because it simply takes missionary one step further. To begin, the woman will lay on her back as usual, and the man gets on top and enters her. Yet, instead of laying down, the man should get onto all fours, and using his hands and knees to essentially propel his penis further into the woman for a deeper penetration. From there, the woman can take over the thrusting and move her hips to meet his body.

Yawning Position

This is another variation of missionary position. Instead of lying over the woman, the man kneels and sits upright as he enters the woman. For leverage, the man and woman press hands together as he thrusts. She can also keep her legs in the air by pressing them against the man's torso.

Splitting Bamboo

This position is very similar to the yawning position, except the man stays on top of one of the woman's legs, while the other is elevated. She puts one leg over one of the man's shoulders, and the man straddles her other thigh, using his hands to support both himself and her elevated leg.

The Curled Angel

Also known as "spooning," this position can be achieved when the woman lies on one side and draws her knees up towards her. The man then enters her from behind. This is an easy pose to initiate, and couples can transition into it directly from cuddling or touching.

Full-Pressed

The full-pressed position, also known as the "piditaka" according to the Kama Sutra, can be wildly stimulating for the woman, due to the angling that's involved. It sounds a bit tricky, but for beginners, it can be much easier if the couple chooses to place a pillow or cushion beneath the woman's lower back for elevation. The woman will be on her back and draw her knees into her chest. The man will then kneel before her and place both of his knees on either side of her hips. The sensation that results from this position can be overwhelmingly pleasurable for both the man and woman, as the vagina will be narrowed due to the elevation.

Cow-Like

This position, called Dhenuka II in the Kama Sutra, is a variation of the classic rear sexual position. The woman will lay face-down, with her legs bent and spread somewhat. The man will extend himself over her body and situate his legs so that they're on the outside of hers. He can then press his pelvis against her rear end and enter her from this position. She can squeeze her legs together for a tighter fit. To achieve a better angle and keep the man from slipping out, you may want to position a pillow under the woman's pelvis.

The Hinge

The hinge position is as the name suggests, the man and woman are interlocked like a hinge during their lovemaking session. This position is a variation of doggy style in which the woman is on all fours, leaning forward onto her elbows and facing away from her partner. The man then sits on his knees and leans backward as he supports his body weight with one arm. Then he places one leg between the woman's legs and enters her, and the woman thrusts back and forth. This is a male dominated position where the male partner has deeper penetration and the woman helps with thrusting. And as the doggy style is, the hinge position has excellent g-spot stimulation.

This position is an alternate to the doggy style position. Like the doggy style, the woman first lies on her knees and arms and faces away from her partner. Then the man kneels and places one thigh between her legs, and penetrates the woman. After he leans back and holds his weight with one arm, he will start to thrust and the woman will also move back and forth.

The hinge position is a primitive position of lovemaking and ensures that the man gets a high degree of satisfaction. There is great friction between the penis and vagina, and the man gets deeper penetration as the woman moves back and forth. She will also have a deeper degree of stimulation due to her g-spot being stimulated and the man's leg being between her thighs.

In this position, the man should not thrust too fast as he can get out of control during sex, and leaning back can break the continuity. He can also get tired of having to hold up his body weight and thrust at the same time.

Proposal Position

This is the position of equals, meaning that both the man and the woman are exactly in the same position. It's a very intimate position and can bring more closeness to couples. In this position, the partners are facing one another, bended on common knee, left or right. By bending the same knees when facing one another and hugging, the opposite knee is going to bend and it will look like they are proposing to one another. The lovemaking is gentle and both partners are not able to stroke fast for a long duration. This is an intimate position where both partners are able to kiss, lick, caress, and touch each other's hips during lovemaking.

To begin lovemaking in this position, both partners should sit on their knees on the bed and face each other. They should be close enough that they are able to hug. Then they should raise their one knee so that the thigh is parallel to the surface of their bed. Their feet should be flat on the ground and the other leg is outside of the other partner's leg. After they are hugging one another and on their knees, the man should penetrate the other woman and stroke gently and slowly. During lovemaking, it will like both partners are proposing to one another but the difference is that they are joined together. Both of them can hold each other's waist to help with the stroking motion.

This position ensures that maximum satisfaction is met by both parties by bringing closeness between the couples. As far as satisfaction is concerned, they can stimulate the pubic areas. The woman can stroke the man's testes and the man can stroke her clitoris during lovemaking. The hands of both partners are free to caress one another.

There are some precautions with this position. If either partner has knee problems, they should avoid this position. It's also not a position to try anal sex in.

The Perch

The perch is a position where the couples will be using a chair. The male partner will sit on the chair and the female partner is going to sit on his lap, facing away from him like a bird on a perch. In this position, she will be perched on top of him, so be sure that both partners are okay with that. The male partner will enter the female partner and then the thrusting will be done by the female partner. The male can hold her hips to either increase or decrease the tempo.

In order to get into the position, the man should sit on the chair with his legs apart and his feet resting on the ground. The woman then perches on his lap and faces away from her partner, bending a little toward the floor so that the man can insert his member into her. Then she will sit upright on his lap and slowly start to move up and down. She can put her hands on the man's thighs to keep herself balanced. She can also push back and forth to change the degree of penetration. The man can speed up the strokes by holding her hips and moving them to increase or decrease the tempo.

When the woman is on top with rear entry, it yields good satisfaction for the woman due to getting sexual gratification and being in charge. She can bend to get the angle she wants and the man has visual stimulation due to the woman being in front of him. The man can reach forward to caress her breasts or hold her behind to keep her steady. The woman can rub her breasts or her clitoris for more arousal.

The female partner can get tired during this position so that male should help during thrusting. The position will definitely yield some stronger thighs for the female partner!

The Grip

The grip is a mix between missionary and the g-force position. In this position, the woman will lie down on her back and raise her lower body above the ground, but instead of resting her legs on the shoulders of the man, she will wrap her legs around the waist of the man, unlike the g-force position. This is a deep penetration position and the woman will experience high g-spot stimulation because she is around the waist of her male partner. This is a good angle for both partners. This is a male dominated position and requires good flexibility, and the woman will need some stamina.

In order to get into this position, the woman will lie down on her back on the bed or a flat surface and her legs will be spread out in the missionary position. The man will sit on his knees in front of her or stand in front of her and hold her waist so that her thighs and lower body are above the ground. He will then bring his pelvis to hers and enter her while she wraps her legs around him at the waist. She will then lock her ankles together to keep him in place. In this position, the man has full leverage because he can change depth and penetration with his partner. The woman has a small role to play, but she does wrap her legs around the man and can thrust up and down during sex, depending on her degree of arousal.

This position allows very deep penetration while the man penetrates the woman from the front and above her body. Due to the clasping position of her legs and her body being raised, there is a lot of g-spot stimulation. The man can thrust himself harder to achieve orgasm, but should be conscious of his partner's level of arousal and comfort. It's a great position for both vaginal and anal sex.

This position should be avoided if the woman has a history of back problems because she could hurt herself.

Balancing Act

This Kama Sutra position originated around 400BCE to 200BCE. The book was written to bring about an entirely new way of life. However, it was more famous for the sex positions that people could experiment with. The book was written in Sanskrit and presented the readers with sixty-nine different positions to choose from.

The balancing act is one of the original positions and ensures that both partners have maximum satisfaction. Both partners have to balance in order to perform this position as well as make the most of it. To start off this position, the man has to lie down on his back with his legs spread wide so that he can accommodate the woman. In the next step, the woman has to sit in between the man's thighs. This is the place where she has to balance. It's actually not as difficult as it sounds.

To get the most out of this position, the man should grip the woman's hips in order to set the rhythm. The woman makes the most of the position by stroking her clitoris or by making an effort to reach down to the man's perineum. This position ensures maximum penetration.

Just be careful with the balancing part as either partner could become injured if one were to slip.

The Slide

This position is where the woman is on top of the man. Men enjoy this position as they like to see women on top and they get to view their genitalia penetrating the woman. The visual scene allows them to become aroused quickly and they gain great satisfaction from it. The slide position is one of the most famous positions where the man will see the woman performing the act of sex. Here, the partner will lie with his back up and the woman will lie on her man, fully nude so that he can see all of her organs. After both the man and the woman feel comfortable, the woman should spread her legs and allow the man to insert his penis into her. She should lubricate her vagina so that the man can easily slide in. Once she feels that she is comfortable, she can close her legs tight and slide her body up and down against her partner.

This position is very much liked by women who like to be on top during sex and allows them to feel dominate. The man feels full penetration and satisfaction while the woman is rubbing her body against his. Be sure that the woman's breasts are touching the man properly so that he can enjoy the feel of her body against his. This is a position where kissing the partner is easy and the woman can play with the man's hair at the nape of his neck, his nipples, and make moaning noises to arouse him further.

While this position is great for sex, the woman should be sure she is positioned comfortably above the male partner. It's also important to be sure that the man does not become crushed or that his genitalia is caught in the process of the motions. Be sure that the man's penis is fully erect before it's inserted or he could pull a muscle. The position is best for women who are lighter than their partner.

The Kneel

In the kneel position, the man and woman sit on each other's laps like a variation of the lotus position. The kneel position is for entertainment, fun, pleasure, enjoyment, delectation, and amusement. It ensures that both partners are being thrilled, desired, and will have an orgasmic experience.

The woman and man kneel in front of one another and she hugs the man. The woman spreads her legs and sits diagonal on the man and puts his genitalia into her vagina. The man and woman move against each other in a rocking motion.

There is satisfaction for both the man and the woman in this position if it's done properly. The man and woman are positioned in a way that they are able to fondle and handle one another or themselves for pleasure. It's a position where they are cozy and intimate and allows for kissing, too.

Some precautions to consider is that if either partner has back problems, this is not a good position for them. Movements must be slow and controlled or the man might slip out of the woman and injure himself. There is no room for wild thrusting in this position, but it can be made up with intimate kissing and whispered words to one another. Be sure to use all parts of your body to make this the most pleasurable position of all!

Close-Up Position

The close-up position is best used for snuggling. It's an intimate and special position that allows the woman to feel the man's body touching her all over, and the skin to skin intimacy will facilitate close bonding. That's why it's called the close-up position!

In this position, the woman will lie on her side in bed while the man will snuggle her from behind. He will embrace her and push himself against her back and she will feel his penis against her tailbone. She will reach back with her hand to stimulate him and caress him until he is aroused. Then she will spread her legs and help him insert himself into her vagina or anus. This position is great for anal sex because it will feel natural. The man should pull his legs together and push himself in and out of the woman. The woman will close her legs on the outside of his legs and hold him inside of her.

This is a very close and intimate position and is sometimes referred to as spooning. The woman can reach down to fondle the man's testes or she can reach down to fondle herself. The man can also reach forward to fondle her breasts or he can reach down to fondle her clitoris. The man can also use both his hands on the woman's breasts. There is also room for kissing if the woman tilts her head back to face the man.

This is a very easy move to perform so there are not any precautions.

Classic

The classic position is a simple position that can be performed by anyone. It's the position where the man and woman are in the primal position they used in nature. The position is both affectionate and aggressive at the same time. The woman lies down on her back and allows the man to penetrate her. Since he is on top, the woman does not have any control in this position. This is also known as the missionary position in the western world.

In this position, there is great satisfaction if the position is performed correctly. It's a position where women will not be in control and will have to take what they are given, but good communication between partners will ensure that it's pleasurable. The man should position his pelvic bone above the woman's clitoris so that she has stimulation and is able to achieve orgasm. He can also hold himself up with one arm and use his free hand to fondle her breasts. There is also a lot of room for kissing and quiet whispering in this position.

The Peg

This position looks very difficult, but it's easily mastered with the right form and figure. First ask the man to like nude with his legs fully stretched out and him on his side. Then the woman curls up on her side the opposite direction of him so that he is able to see her feet and she can see his feet. She then pulls up her knees close to her chest and wraps her thighs tightly around the man's legs. She then holds his legs firmly by wrapping her arms around them. Then the woman asks her partner to support himself on his lower elbow and use his other hand to arouse him and her at the same time. With his free hand, the man can reach out to the woman's anus or vagina and finger either one of them. After both partners are aroused, the woman then has the man lie on his back and she sits on him so that his penis is lined up with her vagina. The woman then thrusts up and down on the man until both reach pleasure.

This is an excellent position to arouse the man because he gets to see the woman fully. The woman can press her own breasts together in order to arouse the man. She can make some moans and a little dirty talk and play with his hair at the nape of his neck. Hair is a very sensitive area and very arousing for men. It's also a great way to kiss and touch each other throughout the experience.

Women should be aware of not putting too much pressure on the man's genitals as this could hurt him. It's also a great position for women to be in control and women can control when a man orgasms. She can slow down when she hasn't reached her pleasure yet and prolong his, and speed up so that both of them get to reach orgasm.

Seduction Pose

This pose is the 'take me now' pose for women. This is where the woman and her partner seduce one another so that they reach the brink of climax. In this position, the woman will lie fully nude with her back on the bed and her arms stretched over her head. Her knees will be stretched up to her stomach so that her vagina is fully exposed, and her partner will be on top kneeling over her. She will widen her legs so that her partner can penetrate his penis inside of her and thrust for satisfaction.

This position ensures satisfaction for both partners. It's also a position that's used in order to get pregnant because the man is able to insert his penis further inside the woman. The woman can also place her legs on the man's shoulders if it's more comfortable. She can apply a little cream or gel around her clitoris so that it is more soft and smooth for the man to enter her. This is a great position because the man gets to see the entire woman's body starting from her breasts, stomach, and to her genitalia.

While this is one of the most commonly followed positions, it is very easy to get pregnant with this position. Those who would like to get pregnant should use it, and those who don't should use protection. The man should be strong enough that he is able to balance on his forearms as the woman does not want him to fall on her with his full weight.

The Star

The star position is like the man on top position, but there is some variation. This position is a combination of the woman lying on her back and the man sitting. In this position, the woman lies on her back as in the missionary position, but one leg is bent and the other leg is stretched out on the bed. The man sits down in front of the woman and who is lying flush on her back with her legs open. Then he slides one leg under her bent leg and the other over her straight leg. In this pose, the man pelvis will hit the lower hip of the woman under her bent leg. This position allows for deep penetration and higher friction for more arousal. The man can also raise the woman's bent leg straight up in the air into the raised legs position, which will increase the stimulation. It's a good and easy position for deep penetration and g-spot stimulation.

To start this position, the woman should lie down flat on her back with her legs outstretched. One leg should be bent at the knee and raised and the other leg should be flat. The man kneels before the woman between her legs. He sits so that one leg is beneath the bent leg and the other leg is over the woman's flat leg. He then thrusts his pelvis against the bent hip of the woman. The man gets deep penetration and excitement, and he has access to the woman's clitoris in this position. In between positions, he can also rub her breasts for more stimulation. The woman also has access to her breasts and clitoris to give the man a visual of her arousal.

This position allows for satisfaction with both partners because the man can thrust as vigorously as he'd like and the woman is able to have her g-spot and clitoris stimulated at the same time.

The Snail

This is a man on top position with a variation of the yawning or crisscross position. In this pose, the woman will lie down on her back on the bed or a mattress with both her legs upright on the shoulders of the man. The different in this pose is that the position if the woman's behind is raised above the bed and held by the man. The raised behind and thighs ensures deeper penetration and quicker climax for the man and woman.

To begin this pose, the woman should lie flat on the bed and raise her legs toward the ceiling. The man should sit on his knees facing his partner. Now the woman can rest her legs on the shoulders of the man and the man will insert himself into her and hold her above the bed by holding her behind or thighs as he thrusts. As the behind and thighs of the woman are raised above the bed, there is deeper penetration for the man. This position can bring higher levels of male arousal and the man will achieve orgasm quickly. It's a good position for fast and rough sex. There is little stimulation for the woman when it comes to the clitoris so she may have to reach down and stimulate herself, as well as stimulate her breasts.

This position ensures there is maximum satisfaction for the man in this scenario because he's getting deeper penetration and more stimulation. The man is also able to change the angle of his penetration by twisting his knees frontward or backward, depending on his level of satisfaction. In this position, there is very little clitoral stimulation so the man can stimulate the woman or she may stimulate herself.

This is a deep penetration move, so the man should be careful not to injure the woman. Otherwise, the position is very easy for both parties to perform and is definitely a beginner's move.

The Hound

This is another rear-entry position where the man is in control. This position looks similar to doggy style but is not quite like it. The woman is bent toward a man or the floor with her hands on the floor and her ankles bent. She then drops herself onto her forearms so that the man can enter her from behind. This position lets the man caress his partner during sex.

The rear entry positions are very stimulating for both the man and woman because deep penetration is achieved. The man can watch the woman's behind and fondle her breasts in this position. It gives a better visual and sensory input for the man than the doggy style position. In this position, the woman will lie down on her knees with her forearms bent and hands equivalent to the ground. This position allows her to support herself using her forearms and her thighs can be spread by the man.

The man then sits on his knees and puts his thighs outside the woman's thighs and penetrates her while he holds her closely. This position is definitely a male dominating position and stimulating for the man due to deep and quick thrusting and stimulating to the woman due to her g-spot being stimulated.

The position allows for satisfaction because the man gets a visual of the woman from behind, and he is able to control the act of intercourse. The woman has satisfaction because the man is holding her during intercourse and he can reach forward to stimulate her. There is also extreme g-spot stimulation for the woman; however, the clitoris is stimulated very little. The woman can raise her lower her behind, changing the angle of penetration for her satisfaction.

If either person has bad knees or lower back problems, this position is not ideal. The man should also be careful not to thrust too hard as the woman is putting her weight on her forearms and this could hurt her.

The Fan

Most positions in the Kama Sutra book are actually based off positions that animals take when they reproduce. Most of them are male dominated positions with the woman being entered from behind, and this position is a lot like that. The fan position has the woman standing with her back to the man as she rests her arms on the back of a chair or on a sofa. The man stands behind her in an upright position, grasps hold of her hips, and begins to thrust. The man can also thrust her back and forth with his hands on her hips. He can also lean over the woman for closer contact and hold her breasts for extra stimulation and arousal. The woman is usually comfortable in this position because she is standing and resting on the back of a piece of furniture.

In order to get into this position, the couple must first choose a chair or sofa that's sturdy, of good height, and great for the bending position. Then the woman will kneel or bend forward over the chair or sofa in order to get into position. After she's leaned on the chair, she will put her legs apart to make it easier for the man to penetrate her from behind. The man penetrates the woman by standing up behind her and holding her waist as he begins to thrust in and out. The man can lean forward and hold her to ensure that there is vigorous thrusting. During intercourse, the man can also hold the breasts of his partner or kiss or lick her neck to stimulate her. The woman can change the angle of penetration by bending forward more or bending back.

To get the best satisfaction out of this position, both partners must be very comfortable. This position has high g-spot stimulation and the friction in this position will increase the woman's arousal. This is a passionate position and lets the male partner achieve higher arousal by stimulating his female partner.

The only precaution is to choose a stool or sofa that's sturdy so that neither partner goes toppling over.

The Clip

This is a variation of the woman on top position and can be done on a smooth surface,

but the bed is the best place for this position. The control is with the woman in this position as she gets to regulate the rhythm and the pace of intercourse. The man can thrust his hips up and down if he does not have back problems or is fit.

To achieve this position, the man should lie down on his back with his legs together. When he is erect, the woman will straddle his hips and guide him into her. Either traditional or anal sex can be achieved in this position. Once the man is inside, the woman will move herself up and down and squeeze her thighs together to provide more friction. The man is able to reach up to fondle the woman's breasts or he can stimulate her clitoris.

This position allows both the man and the woman to obtain pleasure. The woman can reach forward and stimulate her clitoris or her breasts as the man thrusts his hips up and down. Because the woman is on top, gravity takes care of his genitalia staying inside so there is no worry about slipping out. The woman can also reach behind her to caress the man's testes for more stimulation for him. The woman can also lean forward to get closer and kiss the man as well as whisper to him.

There are no precautions with this move as it's very simple to perform.

The Magic Mountain

The magic mountain is a variation of doggy style. There is a pile of cushions or pillows that the woman will lean onto with her front and the man will enter her from behind. The man will enter the woman from behind by bending onto his knees like the doggy style position. It can be different from doggy style because the woman does not have to put her weight on her forearms, so more vigorous thrusting can be achieved. There is also a lot of g-spot stimulation and the man can lean forward to hug the woman from behind to make it more sensual.

To get into this position, there first has to be a mountain of pillows or a beanbag for support for the woman. The mountain should be stable that it can withstand any intense intercourse. After making the mountain, the woman will kneel in front of the mountain and lean forward onto the pile with her arms and shoulders on top of the pillows to hold her weight. The man will kneel on the mattress or bed behind her and rest his weight on his elbows supported by the mountain. The man can also hold the female by her waist to help keep her stable as he thrusts.

To obtain maximum satisfaction, the man should hold the woman from behind and have her lean up a bit so that he can fondle her breasts. He can also reach beneath her to fondle her clitoris. There is a lot of g-spot stimulation in this position, so the man should be careful as to not get too carried away. He may hurt his partner.

Just be sure that the mountain the two partners are leaning on is stable.

The Eagle

This is a basic man on top position. It's similar to the yawning position, but there is a slight variation. The woman's legs are raised high and her thighs are in front of the man. This position is also a variation of the missionary position because the woman raises her thighs and allows them to open while the man sits on his knees and holds her legs while he pushes against her. There is deeper penetration and clitoral stimulation can be achieved in this position.

To get into this position, the woman should first lie down in the missionary position with her back on the bed and her legs and arms straight. The woman spread her legs wide apart and the man kneels in front to penetrate her. He then holds her ankles to keep her in place as he thrusts into her. He can stimulate her manually with his hands or he can lean forward to use his tongue, and she can also stimulate herself with her hands to give the man a show. The woman can vary her stimulation by changing the angle of her thighs and can prolong her thighs behind raised up by pressing them against his body.

The man is in full control of this position and is able to watch the woman enjoy the act, which is a good visual show. The man can also vary the speed.

Deep penetration is achieved during this act so the woman should be fully aroused and lubricated for this position. In addition, the woman can relax her legs by bringing them down every now and again.

The Amazon

The Amazon position is one that is very easy for partners to perform. In this position, the man will sit comfortably on a chair and the woman will sit down on the man facing away from him so that she is straddling him. As long as her feet are touching the ground, she is able to bounce up and down gently. This is an exciting, simple position that anyone can enjoy. The woman can stimulate her breasts or clitoris while the man stimulates her breasts or clitoris, too.

There is a lot of satisfaction in this position as the woman can increase or decrease the tempo and the man can also control the tempo of thrusting by moving his hips or holding the woman's hips and moving her up and down. The position can also be reversed so that the woman is facing the man, that way he is able to stimulate her breasts orally and she can lean her head back to thrust her chest forward for easier access.

The woman should be aware of how hard she is thrusting so that she does not hurt her partner's genitalia.

Chapter 9:
Advanced Positions

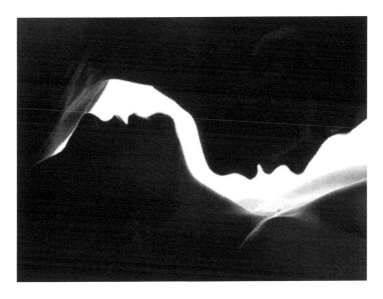

If you've already gone through all of the beginner's positions, or you're simply looking for a bit more of a challenge in the bedroom, you and your partner may want to experiment with some more difficult positions. These can be challenging, so try to approach them with an open mind. As with all other aspects of sexual activity, you and your partner should maintain an open line of communication as you go about experimenting with advanced positions. Take these positions especially slowly, and back off if you experience any pain. These may require some strength and flexibility, but the pleasure that you'll discover once you've achieved these positions will make it worthwhile. Plus, trying something new with your partner promotes bonding, and you'll find that both of you will benefit from the communicative, shared experience of becoming more adventurous in your sex life.

Fixing a Nail

The woman may find that this position will require some flexibility on her part, but it may be worth it to give this an attempt. Called "shulachitak" in the Kama Sutra, this sex position begins with the woman lying on her back. One leg will be stretched up vertically towards her lover's forehead (he will be kneeling around her pelvis). Essentially, the woman will be in a split, and she can rest her foot against his forehead while he penetrates. As he begins, she can alternate legs, so as to change the angle of each thrust. If it seems awkward at first to generate so much movement, consider taking this position a bit slower and moving in a way that's comfortable for both you and your partner.

Suspended Union

The Kama Sutra refers to this position as "sthitarata." In it, both parties will be standing, and it may require some strength from both the male and female. The man will support himself up against a wall, and will lift the woman onto him, holding her by the buttocks. She should then grip his body using her thighs, and her legs and arms will be wrapped fully around his body. If you find this position too difficult at first, consider having the man lean outwards more from the wall with his lower body, so that his pelvis essentially forms a ledge for the woman to sit upon. While this position can be quite invigorating, keep in mind that you don't have to stay in it for a long period of time. You can always experiment and then move on to a simpler position once this becomes too difficult.

The Erotic V

Only the man will be standing for this position. The woman, however, will sit atop a desk or table ledge of appropriate height, and spread her legs. Both legs can be pressed atop the man's shoulders, if the woman is flexible enough to allow for this. Depending on the man's height, he may need to bend his knees slightly to reach the ideal entering position. The woman can lean back to brace herself as he thrusts.

The Catherine Wheel

This position is a bit complex, so take your time setting up for it. To begin, the man and woman should sit opposite one another. Then, the woman can wrap her legs round his torso. The man will then enter her, and while doing so, he can wrap one of his legs over her torso so as to lock her into place. Both parties may have to lean back onto their hands or elbows so as to brace themselves while thrusting.

The Ape

The ape will require some flexibility on the man's part. If he has tight leg muscles, the couple may find this position a bit difficult. Yet, it's not impossible to master, and it can encourage deep penetration. The woman, too, will need a fair amount of strength in order to master this. To begin, the man will lie on his back and draw his knees up towards his chest. From there, the woman will sit backwards on top of him, with his legs still drawn up, and slide him inside of her while propping herself up on his feet. This will require a great deal of balance from both partners. To make things simpler, both he and she can grab one another's wrists or forearms for better balance.

The Double Decker

The double decker is similar to the traditional reverse cowgirl position, in which the woman is atop the man facing towards his feet, only in this position, she leans back towards his chest and props herself up using her elbows. Keeping her knees bent and her feet up on his knees allows for the man to softly penetrate the woman while holding her waist.

Reclining Lotus

This is one of those positions that's in a series of universal missionary positions like the Indrani position. It's a man on top position that has the female partner lying on her back and raising her legs in the air, then crossing them as if she were a lotus flower. The man kneels in front of her and penetrates her from the front. The male partner is the one who will be thrusting and deep penetration will be achieved with this position. The woman can also place a pillow beneath her lower back or behind in order for deeper penetration to be achieved.

The partners should begin in the missionary position. In order to begin, the woman should lie down on her back and raise her legs above the surface, and then cross them. The man then kneels in front of her and penetrates her. Afterward, the man can begin thrusting and can perform a grinding motion in order to stimulate his female counterpart.

This position ensures maximum satisfaction because the male partner is on top. It allows deeper penetration so that the male partner is satisfied, and if the male partner bends forward he can stroke the female partner with his hands. The female partner can increase the depth of penetration by using a pillow behind her and she is able to stimulate her clitoris by reaching between her legs.

Women who are not flexible should avoid this position because they have to keep their legs in the air for the duration of this process. Prolonged sex in this position can also strain her legs and cause pain during or after lovemaking. If the woman is uncomfortable with the full lotus position, she can alternate between the lotus position and the missionary position until she builds up to being able to perform the reclining lotus for the entirety of lovemaking.

The G-Force

The g-force is a gravity defying position and it's also known as the g-spot or the pile driver position. The man is on top where the woman is lying down on her back with only her upper back and shoulder area touching the surface, and her lower back and thighs are in the air. The man holds her thighs to keep her up. This position requires that both partners are flexible and the man is strong. The g-force position is difficult to get into, but it's very arousing and satisfying for both partners. The man gets deep penetration and is able to thrust as fast as he wants, and the woman gets clitoral and g-spot stimulation. It's a good position for both vaginal and anal sex.

To get into the position, the woman lies down on her back and raises her legs into the air and brings them close to her chest. The man kneels in front of her and holds her with her ankles, bringing them close to him. After he holds her ankles, he bends her ankles toward her head and raises her lower back above the surface. Her head and shoulders should be touching the surface and nothing else. After they are in this position, the man penetrates her from the top and holds her ankles. The woman's legs are touching his chest and resting on his shoulders. In this position, the man remains upright during sex. The man enters the woman by pointing his genitals down and begins to thrust. This position has a habit of being uncomfortable for the woman, as she holding herself on her head and shoulders. To balance herself, she can hold the man's thighs during sex.

The pleasure comes from the woman being raised above the ground and her legs behind bent toward her upper body for deep penetration. Because there is deeper penetration, there is more g-spot and clitoral stimulation and both partners are able to achieve orgasm in this position. Women can masturbate in this position by stimulating their clitoris.

Both partners have to be very flexible to perform this position. The man should not thrust too hard or he can strain his genital ligaments and he can injure his partner. If either partner has back problems, they should not perform this position.

The Challenge

This is a male dominant position that is like a variation of doggy style where the woman bends on a chair in a squatting position. The man then bends on his knees to enter her from behind as he holds her thighs. The chair should be a sturdy one as its toppling could injure either partner. This position allows the woman's vagina to be spread apart widely so that the man can easily penetrate her from behind. This allows easy penetration and both the man and the woman can perform thrusting. In this position, the man's job is to get his penis in and out and the female's job is to perform up and down squatting.

In order to perform this position, the woman has to first stand on a sturdy chair in the squatting position. She should be leaning forward toward the b ack of the chair with her elbows and hands on her knees to open up her vagina. The man should stand behind her to enter her from behind and start thrust in and out while holding his partner's hips. He can also wrap himself around her body to obtain greater pleasure and deeper penetration. The woman can squat up and down in order to get better thrusting and deeper penetration.

This position allows for a wider vaginal split so that the man has more pleasure and deeper penetration. It also allows the man to have complete control over penetration so that he is in control. The woman can squat up and down to get more pleasure.

All chair positions are risky, so before getting into the position, be sure the chair is sturdy enough to withhold the woman's weight and the force of the man thrusting. The man should also hold the woman at the waist so that she can maintain balance and he also does not topple over.

Dolphin Pose

The dolphin pose is difficult and should not be tried by everyone. Only those who are physically fit and flexible should try this pose, or it could lead to some injuries for both parties.

This pose is one of the ones that those who practice yoga and acrobatics attempt to try out as it's a position for gymnasts. In this position, the woman will lie down on her back on the bed fully nude. She will have a pillow beneath her head and will push herself gradually to raise her hips and legs toward the ceiling. The woman will have to be good at balancing so that she can balance on her shoulders and keep her neck and head on the bed. The man will place himself between her thighs and adjust himself so that he can insert himself into the woman. He will need to hold the woman's behind so that he is able to support himself and the woman in this position. For even more excitement, the man can lift up the woman's hips so that her leg is not touching the ground. This position is ideal for women who want to become pregnant.

This position allows both partners to come to climax quickly. While the intimacy is not as great as other positions because the body parts are not touching very often, the satisfaction when reaching climax is great. It's a great position to allow the man to reach the woman's g-spot if she requires this type of stimulation. He can also reach one hand forward to stimulate her clitoris, or she can reach up and stimulate her own clitoris during intercourse.

The dolphin pose is very exciting, but do not extend the act because it could lead to some serious consequences for the woman, such as blood clotting in the brain and blackouts for the woman. Her partner should be strong so that he can hold her firmly in position.

Indrani

The Indrani position is a common position practiced in bed. This position should only be performed by those who are fit and flexible.

In this position, the woman will lie down on her back nude on the bed. Her legs will be folded up to her chest. She will clasp her knees tightly so that her privates are exposed. Her partner will then penetrate her from behind. The woman will bring her partner closer by holding his behind tightly from the back and drawing him closer for deeper penetration. The woman should rest her legs in her partner's armpit area and try to push against his chest. In this position, both the man and the woman should be deeply aroused.

To get more satisfaction out of this position, the woman should pull her legs closer to her chest so that the man can penetrate deeper into her. In addition, she can try to move around so that the man can feel himself inside of her. This is an excellent position for both the man and woman to feel one another and see one another at the same time. The man can also fondle the woman with his hands. The woman can also reach the man for maximum pleasure by fondling him.

Arousal and intimacy are increased with this position because the couples are so close to one another. It's a favorite amongst young couples because it does take a degree of flexibility and stamina to perform.

The Ship

This is a woman on top position that is a variation of the cowgirl or rodeo position. In this position, the man lies on the bed and the woman sits on him but she is perpendicular to him, meaning to her legs are on one side of him. The woman is in full control of the tempo and the session, as the man is stable on the bed with his legs stretched out.

To start this position, the man lies on his back and then the woman sits on him and allows him to penetrate her by holding his penis and helping him. The man can bend his knees to ensure that penetration is easier. But instead of facing him or away from him, the woman is showing the man her side. The woman will squat on him with her hands on her knees to balance her weight. The woman can also bend forward with her hands on the bed in order to move up and down. She can rotate to get more arousal, and she can pleasure herself with her hands. She can also vary the depth of penetration by either leaning forward or backward, and the man can bend his knees in order to help the woman with thrusting. He can also reach forward to manually stimulate her clitoris or her breasts. This is a good position for anal sex, but precautions should be taken.

This position with the woman on top allows her to be in control and dominate the situation. She is able to climax easily and quickly while the man's satisfaction can be prolonged.

Precautions for this position include the woman not putting her full weight on the man; the woman should be balancing herself with her hands on her knees or on the bed when she leans forward. The woman should also be light and flexible in order to perform this position.

The Rock n' Roller

This position derives its name from the position the partners are in. In this position, the woman partner will look like she is rolling backward while she is on her back and the man will be rocking her. Therefore, both partners will rock and roll, back and forth, during the duration of the position. This is a variation of the missionary position with a bit more flexibility involved. This position is a male dominant position with the man in control of the penetration and thrusting. The legs of the woman are raised in the air toward her head and her hips are above the ground, which gives her maximum g-spot stimulation. This position is a good position for both partners.

To get started in this position, the woman should lie down on her back in the missionary position and raise her legs in the air. She should then roll them back toward her while she tries to roll back. To roll her legs back, she should put her hands on her hips. The man will then kneel in front of her and penetrate her by gently pushing his pelvis against her hips. Then he can begin to slowly thrust and stroke, and as the man and woman settle in, he can increase the tempo. The man has the full advantage in this position because he is able to hold the woman's legs and thrust harder, and he is able to let her legs go and caress her.

This position with the man on top ensures that both the man and the woman are satisfied. The man is able to obtain deep penetration and thrust quickly while the woman is able to stimulate her breasts and clitoris to achieve climax. She will also have g-spot stimulation in this position.

The woman should be flexible for this position and that's why it's labeled as advanced. She could obtain a neck or back injury during this position if she's not flexible enough. The man should also be aware of his partner's comfort because he can get too carried away with the thrusting in this position.

The Propeller

This position is similar to a propeller moving on a stable platform. In this position, the woman will become the base and the man will play the revolving propeller. To get into this position, the woman will recline onto her back with her legs stretched out. The man will face away from the female partner and lie on her. This is the opposite of the woman on top position where the man will lie down on his back and the woman straddles him with her face away from him. This is an exotic man on top position where the roles are reversed.

To begin this position, the woman will lie down on her back with her legs stretched out. The man will sit on her and face away from her as he leans toward her feet with his legs stretched toward her head. After he's in position, he will penetrate the woman from the top, which can be difficult at the angle he's in. To alleviate this, the woman and raise her hips and widen her legs to let the man insert himself into her. The thrusting is difficult in this position because the man can easily slip out. The man can make circular motions with his hips, which is where the propeller name comes from. During intercourse, the woman can caress the man's behind and help him with propelling motions by holding his hips.

G-spot stimulation and thrusting are very hard in this position so it's more of a pose than a sexual position. The propelling action can create friction between the labia and the penis, which is the only stimulation for the woman.

The man should be careful in this position as his muscles can be strained because of the unusual angle. It can be painful for the man if he tries to thrust during sex.

The Landslide

This is definitely a male dominant position that is difficult to perform. In this position, the woman has very little to do and she is stable during this position. This is a rear entry position, meaning that the woman must lie on her stomach and face the bed with her forearms folded and her face resting on the pillow. The man penetrates her from behind with his legs in front of him and leans back to hold himself up with his hands.

In this position, the man will slide on the woman during intercourse. To begin the position, the woman must lie down on her stomach and stretch her legs straight out for easy penetration. The man sits behind her and puts his legs in front of his body and outside of the woman's body. Then he leans backward in order to penetrate her. After he is inside, the man thrusts slowly and increases speed gradually. The woman can raise her behind or bend her back for deeper penetration, or place a pillow beneath her for a better angle. This position is stimulating for the man.

The position is hard to perform, but the woman's g-spot is fully stimulated because of the odd angle of penetration. The man will enjoy deeper penetration and is able to view the backside of the woman he's with. The woman is immobile during the act and her hips are closer to one another, so she has a higher degree of pleasure due to the pressure. She can also bring her legs closer for a higher degree of friction.

In this position, the man has to be careful with leaning back because he could hurt his genitalia. To avoid this mishap, he can change the depth of penetration by leaning forward during intercourse.

The Crossed Keys

In this position, the legs of the woman will remain crossed during intercourse. This is a male dominated position where the woman will lie on her back with her legs crossed and facing the ceiling. The man will enter her from the front while he holds onto her legs. This is a deep penetration position and the man has a high degree of sexual satisfaction compared to his partner. There is less eye contact as the woman's legs are going to be in front of the man during intercourse.

The woman should lie on her back on a bed or on a flat surface and raise her legs toward the ceiling, and the man will enter her from the front while he sits on his knees and holds her legs. In this position, there is a lot of friction between the woman and the man's genitalia as the woman's vagina will become tight due to her legs being crossed. Another option is to have the woman lie on her back with her legs raised and crossed before the man penetrates her, but she must be fully lubricated for this position. After penetration, the man may thrust as light or hard as he wishes and the woman doesn't have a lot of control over the depth or the thrusting.

In order to ensure maximum satisfaction for both partners, the man can raise the woman's behind and vary the angle of penetration by increasing or decreasing the level at which her legs are crossed. The woman's stimulation is not very much so she should stimulate her breasts to get satisfaction.

This position has a lot of deep penetration, so the man should take care not to thrust too hard or deep if the woman is not fully aroused yet. There should be a lot of lubrication to ensure the woman is comfortable. The man should continue to hold the woman's legs in order for her to not become strained.

Suspended Scissors

Suspended scissor is difficult for the partners to get into, so beginners should avoid this pose because it could cause injury. This position requires that both partners are athletic and fit. To begin the position, the man will stand firm and hold the woman's waist to support her weight. She will put one hand on the floor or bed and hold the arm of the man with the other hand. She will then put her legs by the side of her partner and one leg will intersect with her partner's leg. This position will keep penetration at a different angle and make it more exciting and comfortable.

Before trying this position, both partners should be fit. Those who have high blood pressure should avoid this position. Those who have knee or muscle injuries should avoid this position.

Bonus Master Move: The Bridge

This position is ideal for a quick - very quick, in fact - lovemaking session. It requires a great deal of strength, flexibility, and balance on the man's part, and may be best performed on a bed or other soft surface. That way, no one will get hurt if the man needs to come out of the position. To start, the man will create a bridge with his body (also known to yogis as a full-wheel backbend) and the woman will straddle him in this position, moving herself up and down. To take the weight off of him somewhat, she should support herself with her feet while doing so. Don't stay in this position too long, though - while it's difficult to hold in the first place, it can also create dizziness for the man from all of the blood rushing to his head.

Conclusion

While many believe that the Kama Sutra is all about sex, it goes deeper than that because it encourages couples to communicate, bond, and try new experiences together. In doing so, loved ones can maintain a high level of passion, even in relationships that have lasted for many years. Even if you and your partner are sexually satisfied, there's always room to try new things and achieve a greater level of intimacy.

As you enhance your sexual repertoire, you'll likely find that the passion you achieve in the bedroom will transcend into other aspects of your life. Couples that are intimate and sexually satisfied tend to have a healthier relationship overall. Maintain communication with your loved one, not just inside of the bedroom, but in all aspects of your relationship. Communication, compromise, and a passionate sense of intimacy are all essential for a healthy, happy relationship. Of course, don't forget to have fun, and approach the Kama Sutra with a positive attitude, and be open to all of the things that you may discover while exploring your loved one in the most intimate ways possible.

Finally, if you enjoyed this book, please take the time to share your thoughts and post a review on Amazon. We do our best to reach out to readers and provide the best value we can. Your positive review will help us achieve that. It'd be highly appreciated!

BONUS

Tantric Massage For Beginners

Discover The Best Essential Tantric Massage- and Tantric Love Making Techniques !

R. Riley

Table of Contents

Introduction

Tantric sex is a practice that has been around for a very long time, but it's finally making its way into Western culture. It was first introduced by sex therapists who wanted to help their patients grow closer together after a long period of not being intimate, and has long since been incorporated into many bedrooms across the nation. This new method of having sex focuses on both partners' emotional, physical, and mental arousal during sex. In Western culture, physical arousal is about the only thing focused upon, which can lead to a very dry, boring experience for the female partner, and sometimes the male partner, too.

Tantric sex has been proven to help partners increase their desire for sex and their desire for one another. It is able to bring partners closer together both in the bedroom and outside of it. Mental connection between partners is just as important as emotional and physical connections during intercourse.

So if you're looking for a way to increase your enjoyment during sexual intercourse and when you're spending free time with your partner, take a look at this book to see if it can help you!

Chapter 1:
What is Tantric Sex

Tantric sex is a practice that has been happening for over 6,000 years in India. Eastern cultures adopted it due to the overwhelming amount of religions stating that sexuality was something to be rejected in order to reach enlightenment. This practice challenged the beliefs of the time and preached that sexuality was, in fact, a doorway to the divine and earthly desires such as eating, creative expression, and dancing were all sacred acts.

The word tantra translates to 'to manifest, to show, to weave, and to expand'. In the context of tantric sex, the word stands for sex expanding the consciousness and weaving together the polarities of the male and female bodies and minds into a harmonious whole.

However, couples do not have to adopt the belief system of tantric sex in order to benefit. The practice simply teaches couples to prolong their acts of making love and to utilize their orgasmic energies in a more effective manner. Tantra is also known as health enhancing.

So how is tantric sex exceptional?

Well, in Western culture, we usually view sex as recreation rather than transformation. The goal of sex is usually to pleasure ourselves rather than our partner, and we're almost never focused on connecting with our partners on a deep, emotional level. The Western culture's idea of lovemaking has a beginning and an end with a climax somewhere in between for the woman and a climax at the end for the man. It usually lasts around ten to fifteen minutes, even though a woman can take about twenty minutes to reach full arousal. For women, this type of sex can be deeply unsatisfying.

Tantric sex uses the sexual experience more like a dance where it has no beginning or an end. There isn't any specific goal, only the current moment of having sex. Sex is more like meditation and is very communicative and close. Tantra teaches a couple how to extend their sexual ecstasy peak and allows both men and women to have several orgasms in a single encounter.

Even men who experience premature ejaculation are able to extend their orgasms and even enjoy multiple orgasms with practice! And who doesn't like to practice?

To find out how you can supercharge your sex life and bring intimacy back to the bedroom, read further!

Chapter 2:
Beginning Exercises

When you first begin tantra, you may not experience an orgasm for a few weeks. That's because these following exercises are all about reconnecting with your partner rather than actually performing the act of sex. These steps are meant to teach you that intercourse is not the ultimate goal and that giving and receiving pleasure using gentle touches and loving words is the goal.

As you're performing these exercises, communicate with your lover to figure out what they find most arousing. For many couples, performing these exercises help lovers forget about the pressure of going all the way and allows them to release sexual guilt, build up trust and reawaken their sexual desires.

Welcome Love

The first step to this exercise is to make time for each other every week. Plan a time where the two of you will be intimate at least once a week and set aside an hour or more of uninterrupted time to just be together. Your relationship has to be a priority, so if you have to find someone to babysit children, then find that person.

The second step is to create an inviting atmosphere. You don't have to meet in your bedroom. You could meet up in the living room, kitchen or even the bathroom for a tub date! Just be sure to light some candles, lay out some fresh flowers, find some finger foods to enjoy together, enjoy a few pieces of erotic art, and light some incense for an erotic aroma. You don't have to go all out though. You could just dim the light and play a little erotic music in order to create a welcoming environment.

The third step is to dress daringly, or wear nothing! You should experiment with clothing and accessories that make you feel erotic, as well as turn your partner on.

Intimacy Exercises

When you first start out with the intimacy exercises, you want to start with a ritual. This can something a simple as sitting and gazing into each other's eyes or feeding each other finger foods. You can even share a glass of wine nude, or bathe together in order to be in tune with each other.

Take the time to wash each other, feed each other, and listen to each other speak as you talk about your day or talk about things you enjoy. Even if it's something you may have talked about before, we oftentimes forget what our partners enjoy in life and need a good refresher.

Next, massage each other or read to each other. Dance and play music or sing together. Do something together that makes you fuse your energies and develop some new intimacy skills. Use the time you have together in order to communicate and share what you like about each other. You're aiming to help your partner feel loved and cherished, and understood, above all else.

This is where it gets tricky. Some will choose to perform these rituals for only a week while others may choose to perform this ritual for a few months before they actually hit the sack together. This is a personal choice and this step should never be rushed! After all, if you're a couple who has been at rock bottom for a few years, it could take up to six months before the two of you feel you can trust each other again. Intimacy takes time, and when it's a matter of the heart, it shouldn't be rushed.

Deep Breathing Exercise

Breathing is something we usually don't think about doing unless we're having some serious trouble doing it, so when you consciously breathe, you become much more aware of your surroundings and who you're with. So try this exercise with your partner.

Sit quietly with your legs crossed and face each other. Place your hand son your knees with your palms facing up and gaze into your partner's eyes. Take very soft, deep breaths as you each gaze at one another, and then try to gaze beyond the eyes but into the soul. This may feel very awkward and you both may find yourselves smiling as you do this, but just keep your gazes fixed and refrain from speaking. Eye contact is essential for intimacy to be built up.

Pay special attention to your breathing as you perform this exercise. Breathe at the same pace as your partner, bringing air slowly in through the nose and exhaling through the mouth. Remember to maintain eye contact as the two of you breathe together. Practice until the two of you can keep eye contact and breathe at the same time for a total of ten minutes. Then move to the next exercise.

Erotic Touch

This experiment takes place as you're both practicing the eye contact exercise, but synchronized breathing is not as essential to this step. Your breath will come back into the picture later on. Guide your partner as you take turns stimulating each other and describe how you want to be touched.

Share your desires in a positive manner and make requests in a clear but loving manner. Ask your lover to caress an erogenous zone and encourage them to apply more or less pressure. Let them know if you want them to use a specific pattern or if you want them to use their tongue or another part of their body. Thank them and allow them to know that you are enjoying their sensual touches.

When the two of you are comfortable with this, you may want to create a pleasure chest. Add toys that excite you and your partner such as a feather, some massage oil, a vibrator, some soft fabric, a blindfold, or maybe some erotic notes or cards. As you pleasure each other, do not ever feel ashamed to ask for something different. This is a time for experimentation, appreciation, and taking responsibility for your own fulfillment rather than letting your partner stumble around in the dark.

From this exercise, you should take it to the next level and create adventures together. Explore the new and creative ways you can awaken each other. Then, and only then, will you be able to enjoy and practice tantric lovemaking properly.